PROMOTING READING TO ADULTS IN UK PUBLIC LIBRARIES

Margaret Kinnell and Jennifer Shepherd

British Library Research and Innovation Report 72

TAYLOR GRAHAM

Published by

Taylor Graham Publishing
500 Chesham House
150 Regent Street
LONDON W1R 5FA
United Kingdom

Taylor Graham Publishing
12021 Wilshire Boulevard
Suite 187
LOS ANGELES, CA
90025
USA

ISBN 0 947568 74 3

RIC/G/336

ISSN 1366-8218

Contents

This report discusses the findings of the British Library Research and Innovation Centre investigation into how libraries are promoting reading to their adult users. Based at the Department of Information and Library Studies, Loughborough University, from 1996-1997, the research focused on adults' reading for leisure, pleasure and informal education, and covered library services throughout the UK. As well as providing up-to-date information on the present state of reading promotion policies and practices, the research brought together a wide range of expert views on the potential for improvement. Other research and writing on reading promotion was also used to inform the discussion and recommendations.

The authors

Margaret Kinnell (Evans) is Head of the Department of Information and Library Studies, Loughborough University, and Professor of Information Studies. She has a special interest in the management of change in public sector services and has undertaken several investigations in the public library field. She also researches and teaches in the field of childhood and children's literature and is managing editor of the *New Review of Children's Literature and Librarianship*. Other publications include *Continuity and innovation in the public library* (Library Association Publishing) and *Managing fiction in libraries* (Library Association Publishing).

Jennifer Shepherd has recently retired from the post of Assistant Director of Leicestershire Libraries and Information Service, where she had responsibility for a wide range of services, including services to children and education, adult stock, publicity and promotion, information services, bibliographical services and special services. She was a member of the senior management team and was also responsible for the successful Leicestershire Fiction Festival. Before that she worked in Shropshire as County Children's Librarian, in Buckinghamshire and in Leicester City Libraries.

Acknowledgements

We should like to record our thanks to all who gave their time and expertise to this study through consultation and interviews, and especially to those senior librarians who completed the questionnaires at a point when local government reorganisation was creating many more demands on their time.

The project was funded by the British Library Research and Innovation Centre, and we are particularly grateful for the support we received from John Burchell and Isobel Thompson, and Carolyn Pritchett, who undertook much valued work on the questionnaire survey.

1. Introduction

This is the final report of the Promotion of Reading to Adults in Public Libraries project which was funded by the British Library, Research and Innovation Centre and took place between June, 1996 and June, 1997. The project was based at the Department of Information and Library studies, Loughborough University and directed by Margaret Kinnell Evans. Jennifer Shepherd was the research co-ordinator and Caroline Pritchett provided research assistant support.

1.1 Definitions

1.1.1 Focus

The project focused on how public libraries are promoting reading to their adult users. The concern was with the general adult reader. Literacy students, those with special needs and adults pursuing a course of formal education did not come within the specific remit of the investigation although, inevitably, library policies and programmes which develop reading within the community have potential to benefit every user. The aim was to look at adults' reading for leisure, pleasure or informal education.

1.1.2 Promotion

This is defined as any means by which libraries encourage people to read or to widen their reading horizons. How the library takes a proactive role in advising or encouraging their readers in what to read - widening their horizons or simply making it easy for them to make choices - was our concern. We were therefore interested in methods such as alternative forms of arrangement including categorization, 'dump bins', displays; promotional materials such as book-lists and posters; reading groups; author events; and in ideas for using the knowledge and passions of readers to pass on their enthusiasms to their co-readers. There were many issues underpinning promotion which had to be considered. These included library policies and plans and the structures, staffing and resources which supported this work and in the collaboration or support which libraries had gained in spearheading such developments either singly or in consortia with the co-operation of library suppliers or bookshops, or the Arts Council.

1.1.3 Scope

The scope of materials considered was broadly interpreted: fiction of all kinds including, but not concentrating exclusively on literature (however this may be defined), genre fiction, modern contemporary novels and all types of non fiction.

1.2. Objectives

The objectives of the project were :

a. to draw together findings from user studies and reader surveys which have relevance to the promotion of adult reading /literature in public libraries;
b. to identify the state of the art in public libraries with regard to policies, strategies and programmes, to identify how reading needs are ascertained and to aid reading promotion programmes;
c. to identify the relative importance, motivation, training and expertise accorded to these areas by library management and librarians working in public libraries, and to explore the current initial and continuing educational training being provided and the potential for development;
d. to identify any constraints which mitigate against successful promotional programmes;
e. to identify policies and strategies in the book trade which relate to these issues and, where possible, identify criteria for successful promotion as it impacts on public libraries;
f. to identify the policies and strategies of the Arts Council which have been influential in encouraging libraries to develop reading promotion;
g. to propose appropriate ways forward which would encourage the development of reading promotion for adult users as a core activity in public libraries.

1.3 Research focus

The research focus was on England, Scotland, Wales and Northern Ireland. The timing of the project was particularly significant: local government reorganization of Scotland and Wales was taking place in 1996 and of England in 1997 - with planning for 1998 under way in some local authorities. This inevitably meant that many library authorities were more than usually pressurised and some were so new that basic service policies had yet to be formulated. This was a difficulty in one way but conversely an advantage in that many authorities were at a point of change, causing them to rethink policies and strategies and the particular emphasis for their new services. We were indeed thanked by more than one authority for raising the issues at this particular time.

1.4 Timeliness and significance of the project

This is the first major study of reading promotion for adult readers in the UK. There were very few references in the literature which took an overview of the role of public libraries specifically in reading promotion. Most references related to individual schemes, for example, the work of Sear and Jennings[1] and Goodall[2] on browsing and the 'Well Worth Reading' scheme.[3] There is a great deal of material on fiction in public libraries, reflecting the ongoing debate about 'fiction on the rates', particularly work by Kinnell[4] and Spiller[5], with some of the concerns of these sources moving from selection and acquisition to promotion. We found no significant investigation which had focused primarily on the wide-ranging issues associated with the promotion of reading for adults, other than the brief library survey undertaken in June, 1996 by the National Literacy Trust. This asked about activities which involved reading and writing for pleasure, and offers short annotations describing their initiatives from those authorities who responded. It is interesting as an overview but provides no analysis, explanation or contact details.[6]

The majority of individual authorities' promotional schemes are fiction orientated, perhaps because of the strong influence of the Arts Council. There is a good deal of material on the promotion of library services as a whole - some of which takes in elements of reading promotion. Of these there were examples of book promotion which deserve further dissemination in this report as they also supported our consideration of the relationship between reading for pleasure and the developing role of the public library: e.g. R. Van Riel and O. Fowler. *Opening the book: finding a good read.* Bradford: Bradford Libraries, 1996, 127pp, ISBN 0 907734 47 2.

Designed as a guide for readers, it offers an analysis of the reading process, and provides both an explanation of the act of creative reading and a justification for the role of libraries in supporting all kinds of reading and writing.

> *Reading is a creative act. You can be transported to the furthest reaches of the galaxy without leaving the comfort of your armchair; you can make expert analysis of*

forensic evidence in a murder investigation... You are involved in a creative partnership with the author. Your part in the book is as important as the writer's because without your contribution the author can't make theirs.[7]

Definitions of types of reader, from 'thrill seeker' through to 'the indulgent reader' may not be grounded in empirical evidence, but the descriptions are apt and enable individuals to reflect on their reading behaviours which, as this report highlights, may change from day to day and from one setting to another.

R. Huse and J. Huse, comps. and eds. *Who else writes like? A readers' guide to fiction authors.*2nd ed. Loughborough: Loughborough University Library and Information Statistics Unit, 1996. 293pp. ISBN 0 948848 84 7

This edition of the guide which was first published in 1985 contains over 1,200 entries, including 50 authors and titles of books for teenagers. Many library authorities were involved in the compilation and its popularity as a tool for both librarians and readers is undoubtedly due to the profession's 'ownership' of the work. The inclusion of a select list of further guides and bibliographies for fiction is an additional asset.[8]

1.5 Rationale

For many years public library services have identified the promotion of reading for children and young people as one of their prime aims. Recent reports and government policy have confirmed this key role and have provided much of the rationale for the present project.
The Review of Public Libraries report stated that

One significant outcome of our research has been the strong feelings expressed about the importance of the public library for children and young people... It is therefore heartening to see an investment in the young at the head of a list of prime purposes at the core of the public library services.[9]

The Library and Information Services Council (England) Report, *Investing in children,* reinforced this message:

...it is our clear view that, at a time when unfulfilled reading potential affects the economic, cultural and social life of the country, the potential of a library and in particular the public library, which is fully available to all, as a force in support of reading and information literacy cannot be too strongly emphasised.

...The promotion of books and the enjoyment of reading is an integral and vital part of the public libraries' service to children and young people.[10]

The summary of the Review of Public Libraries report had little to say on the promotion of reading to adults. It did however find from a variety of sources that :

> *...popular reading is a broadly based concept and one with a sustained and increasing hold on people's leisure time... Library users, from our research, seek out a wide range of material not merely the superficial. According to students of reading habits people borrow fiction mainly for recreational purposes. However there is a body of research which reinforces the common sense view that borrowers of fiction also derive other worthwhile benefits from their reading; in particular the factual content of novels often helps to inform readers.* [11]

The Review defined the supply of a range of popular reading materials (broadly defined) as one of libraries' [12] core functions but found that the marketing of services was deficient. As had been found in previous work [12], 'many library staff see marketing as primarily advertising' rather than as a total marketing approach which encompasses the library environment, planning services and public relations. Much work needed to be done in this area. However, the Review Report had little to say on how this marketing should be achieved or what constituted public libraries' proactive role in promoting reading or the dilemma posed between satisfying demands (possibly for the latest blockbuster or for genre fiction) and the development of a more informed and possibly more satisfied public through reading promotion.

The Library and Information Commission was set up in 1994 with a wide-ranging brief, as a national focus of expertise to advise the government on co-ordination of policies, represent UK interests internationally and maximise benefits from available resources by encouraging cooperration and co-ordination. Its 20/20 Vision Statement, published in early 1997, sets out to articulate the Commission's vision of the value of library and information services, and to provide a framework for the Commission's work in encouraging government to demonstrate the value of libraries in economic, educational and social policy terms. [13] It shows libraries as essential for the memory of society and in providing citizens with opportunity for life-long learning, access to knowledge and works of creative imagination and individual empowerment. The Advisory Council on Libraries was set up at the same time to replace the Library and Information Services Council, England (LISC). It has a remit concerned largely but not solely with public libraries and assumes the role of LISC (advising the Secretary of State on responsibilities for public libraries in England, the allocation of direct grants, issues affecting providers and users of English public libraries and which aspects of services require investigation). There is therefore a continuing commitment at national level to develop and support policy and practice in public library provision and a consequent need to identify the means of achieving the full potential of library services in promoting reading.

This had also been identified as an issue in the Comedia study of public libraries, whose report, *Borrowed time,* drew attention to the threat to libraries of quality book shops which developed during the 1980s:

> These tastefully and expensively fitted out bookstores, and their enthusiastic and dedicated staff, have espoused the cause of modern literary fiction with a vengeance, making the public library look even more behind the times than ever.

The report also identified that, while most libraries undertake some promotion, bookshops 'now seem to do it better'.[14] In the course of the Comedia study a series of working papers was commissioned, one of which, *Working paper 5: Reading promotion schemes,* is of particular relevance to this study. Noting that *'many of the original functions of the public library have perhaps in a relatively affluent consumer society, been taken over by commercial bookselling'* it advocated co-operation rather than competition but also stated that it was not until the 1980s that libraries began to look seriously at promotion as librarians - with few exceptions - are not instinctive marketers.[15]

In recent years, the Arts Council has been particularly influential in supporting and enabling libraries to become more active in literature promotion. However, in 1989, when *The glory of the garden* was published, a proposal for the future development of the Arts in Great Britain, a deliberate policy to exclude literature was put forward on the basis that public libraries and bookshops were already doing all that was necessary and the somewhat surprizing statement was made that 'the Council finds it difficult to satisfy itself of the value of much of its present support for literature'.[16] Thus for several years literature took a low priority in the Arts Council's activities. However, pressure from the Regional Arts Boards reversed this policy and a conference was held in York in 1992 which was hailed as 'bringing a sea change in the status of literature within the public library service'. Many of the developments of the last five years can be accredited to the library fund innovation scheme which was launched at that event, as we consider in depth in Chapter 3.[17]

1.6 The changing role of public libraries

Most of the promotion undertaken by public libraries in recent years has been concerned with the promotion of services rather than with one of their basic products: books and reading. The greatest concern over this period has been that non-users should be informed of the range of services which are available. In developing the proposal for this present study, we found that there was a considerable momentum to reconsider the core concern of the library's role as a provider of books for pleasure. There was a need to get back to the roots of public librarianship - evident in many of the recent studies of public library services. The changing role of the public library may be summed up in the following chronology:

1. The early days from the 1850s to the end of the nineteenth century when the library was clear in its role as agent to meet the needs of working class literacy and self-education.
2. The development of the county library service in the 1920s following the 1919 Public Libraries Act and the development of a strong middle class clientele.
3. The post -war increase in library building and a widening of libraries' role to take on cultural activities.
4. The 1960s, the 'golden age of children's literature', and the interaction of children's librarians with authors, publishers and their young readers.
5. The 1970s, when the attention turned to adult literacy and a new function for library involvement and support; the development of community librarianship and an emphasis on special services.
6. The impact of the 1974 local government restructuring when many library services were absorbed into larger departments, often leisure directorates.
7. The growing impact of new technology in the 1980s and 90s, initially as a housekeeping mechanism and gradually made available to library users.
8. The present funding and identity crisis with threats of charging for services, compulsory competitive tendering and now 'best value', further reorganization and budgetary problems.
9. Almost full circle to a new interest in reading and reading promotion which has lain dormant for some years.

1.7 Research elements

The rationale shows that the research for this project was concerned not only with describing what is happening in libraries now but in seeking to establish trends and also reasons and explanations for what has happened in the past. It was therefore necessary to combine several different research methods in order to cover the following elements in the study:

a) identifying the present state of the art of reading promotion, including significant or interesting development work;

b) gathering the opinions and comments of key people who would be able to offer explanations for what is happening in public libraries today and develop a vision for the future.

1.7.1 Methods

1. A survey of all public library authorities in England and Wales, Scotland and Northern Ireland was carried out in October/November, 1996, by means of a postal questionnaire The questionnaire instrument is reproduced at Appendix A. The response rate from the questionnaire was 83%. The survey findings are discussed at appropriate points within the report. A further 10% of the respondents was contacted by telephone to elicit further information concerning their replies.

2. In-depth interviews were conducted with individuals who had a particular interest or responsibility in this area from libraries, the arts and the book trade. These included:

Susie Brain, *Director, Library Services, UK*
Alison Dunn, *Literature Development Worker, Leicestershire*
Professor Judith Elkin, *Head of Department, School of Information Studies, University of Central England*
Debbie Hicks, *Literature and Visual Arts Officer, East Midlands Regional Arts Board*
Grace Kempster, *Chief Librarian, Leeds City Council*
Miranda McKearney, *Independent Consultant*
Alaistair Niven, *Director of the Arts Council of England, Literature Department*
Colin Orr, *Manager, Waterstones Bookshop, Leicester*
Ross Shimmon, *Chief Executive, The Library Association*
David Spiller, *Director, Library and Information Statistics Unit, Loughborough University*
Verna Taylor, *County Librarian of Northamptonshire and a member of the Literature Panel of the Arts Council of England*
Dr B. Usherwood, *Reader, Department of Information Studies, Sheffield University*
Rachel Van Riel, *Independent Consultant*

The format of the interview varied according to the background or specialisation of the interviewee.

3. A *pro forma* letter /questionnaire was sent to the 10 Literature Officers at the Regional Arts Boards and The Welsh, Scottish and Northern Ireland Arts Councils.

4. A number of other agencies and individuals were contacted for information on their activities and views, including:

The Book Trust
Book Trust Scotland,
The Scottish Arts Council
The Scottish Library Association
The National Literacy Trust.
*Pearl Valentine, Chief Librarian, North Eastern Education and
        Library Board, Northern Ireland*

5. An interim dissemination and data-gathering seminar was held in April 1997. Thirty-one participants were invited, including all of those who had taken part in the interviews or in the follow up telephone interviews. The purpose was to gain further first -hand experience of public library initiatives and librarians' views and to facilitate discussion between the project participants, including members of the book trade and the arts sector. It was also seen as important to encourage participants to challenge our preliminary conclusions and recommendations. The results of the seminar discussions are included as part of the content of this report.

References

1. SEAR, L. *and* B. JENNINGS. *How readers select fiction. Kent County Council library research and development report.* Maidstone: Kent County Council, 1986.

2. GOODALL, D. *Browsing in public libraries.* Loughborough: Library and Information Statistics Unit, Loughborough University, 1989.

3. MCKEARNEY, M. Well Worth Reading: fiction promotion scheme comes of age. *Public Libraries Journal,* 5(3) 1990, 61-67.

4. KINNELL, M. ed. *Managing fiction in public libraries*, London: Library Association Publishing, 1991.

5. SPILLER, D. The provision of fiction for public libraries, *Journal of Librarianship,* 12(4) 1980, 226-38.

6. NATIONAL LITERACY TRUST. *Database and information service: library survey.* London: National Literacy Trust, 1997.

7. VAN RIEL, R. *and* O. FOWLER. *Opening the book. Finding a good read.* Bradford: Bradford Libraries, 1996, 13.

8. HUSE, R. *and* J. HUSE, comps . and eds. *Who else writes like? A readers' guide to fiction authors.* 2nd ed. Loughborough: Loughborough University Library and Information Statistics Unit, 1996.

9. ASLIB. *Review of the public library service in England and Wales for the Department of National Heritage.* London: Aslib, 1995, 191.

10. LIBRARY AND INFORMATION SERVICES COUNCIL (ENGLAND) *Investing in children.* London: HMSO, 1995.

11. ASLIB. *Review of the public library service in England and Wales for the Department of National Heritage.* London: Aslib, 1995, 185-6.

12. KINNELL, M. *and* J. MACDOUGALL. *Meeting the marketing challenge: strategies for public libraries and leisure services.* London: Taylor Graham, 1994.

13. LIBRARY AND INFORMATION COMMISSION. *2020 vision.* London: LIC, 1997.

14. COMEDIA. *Borrowed time? The future of public libraries in the UK.* Stroud, Glos: Comedia, 1993, 74.

15. WORPOLE, K. *The public library and the bookshop.* Working paper 3, Stroud, Glos: Comedia, 1993.

16. ARTS COUNCIL OF GREAT BRITAIN. *The glory of the garden: the development of the arts in England: strategy for a decade.* London: Arts Council of Great Britain, 1984.

17. VAN RIEL, R. *Reading the future; a place for literature in public libraries. A report of the seminar held in York, March, 1992, organised by the Arts Council of Great Britain in association with the Library Association.* London: Arts Council, 1992.

2. The service environment and the public library's role in reading promotion

In this chapter, we consider the context within which library services are being delivered and the policies and service structures which are relevant to reading promotion. A central issue is the extent to which resources and professionalism are being sufficiently directed towards this key public library function in a turbulent local authority setting.

2.1 The political context

In assessing the public library's role in promoting reading we found it necessary to re-visit the service environment, and to consider its impact over the past twenty years on the meeting of core objectives, given that literature promotion should be at the heart of these. It could be argued that turbulence and rapid changes have deflected attention from the key aspects of public libraries' mission.

> The world of local government is in a turmoil, during the 1980s no fewer than 124 Acts of Parliament had direct or indirect bearing on local government.[1]

In surveying these changes in light of this project, we found that their scale had impacted profoundly on public libraries and the way in which their core service was being delivered. In 1974 in England and Wales, although many of the smaller authorities were swallowed up by reorganization and deeply regretted their loss of independence and locality, the general mood was one of optimism. The new larger authorities had more adequate funding and the prospect of developing services. Writing in 1977, Kelly reflected on over a hundred years of public library history and found much expansion of information services, despite the concern at falling issue figures for adult fiction and children's books in the period 1970-75.[2] Services were being delivered in a relatively stable context which engendered hopes that continuing expansion would be feasible.

The situation changed rapidly from 1979 when the incoming government delivered a range of measures which impacted on the powers of local authorities, although from 1987 the government instead of attempting to exert control over local authority spending through legislation used the concept of market forces. The local authority was no longer the only provider of services; as an enabling authority it had the responsibility of contracting for services, and monitoring their delivery, and for this was accountable to the local electorate. It was during the '80s that right- wing think-tanks such as the Adam Smith Institute developed the idea that local government should not merely be business-like but operate as a business. The local authority would be:

> as only one of a number of suppliers, contracting out to other agencies and the private sector to produce and deliver services. It will be customer centred, seeking to understand its customers and clients, responding to the electorate and identifying and serving community needs.[3]

The Local Government Act, 1988, brought in compulsory competitive tendering for specified services and the potential for this was explored for others. The 1988 Education Reform Act and the Housing Act of 1988 allowed for opting out of local government control and in some authorities departments traded internally with a purchaser-provider split. Within this context, it was inevitable, therefore, that much of the energy and vision of library managers and their committees was directed towards survival - through restructuring, the deployment of new management techniques and responses to government reviews.

Librarians had viewed the Government's edict on compulsory competitive tendering (CCT) with some foreboding. In 1994, the Department of National Heritage asked KPMG and Capital Planning Information to undertake a study on contracting out [4] Their conclusions were that the introduction of CCT for libraries was feasible but that there was not then a sufficiently developed external market. The Secretary of State issued a statement in December 1995 ruling out the introduction of CCT for the present, but stressing that authorities should strive to improve their management and effectiveness by involving the private and voluntary sectors.[5] (Best value is now the initiative which will be used to market test library services. Pilot projects were introduced in 1997).

There were even more wide-ranging concerns when local government boundaries again came up for consideration, as a consequence of government dissatisfaction with the complexity of the structures introduced in 1974. The 1974 reorganization had left a two-tier structure which applied to most of the UK but this was viewed as too complex for the electorate who were unsure of which authority to go to for a response; and there were said to be political tensions between the two levels. The subsequent restructuring of local government, which is now almost completed, has therefore resulted in further changes to the service context. From 1992, the review established to look at local government considered finance, the internal management of local government and the structure of local authorities. Since the 1997 Election, there has been further interest in local structures, with regionalism now a major issue. The potential for further regional collaboration between library services, perhaps reviving the regional library bureaux concept, is therefore another element which library authorities will need to assess as they develop the plans which the Department of Culture, Media and Sports requires library services to deposit annually.

2.2 Change and public library development

2.2.1 Service development

These changes and the climate of continual flux have had a considerable impact on all public library services, as we found in the questionnaire responses. The various reorganizations have inevitably meant that much time which would have been used in providing services has been absorbed into restructuring to meet new geographical boundaries or changed management structures.

> *Local government changes have had a destructive effect in Wales providing services which are too small, under resourced, lacking corporate influence and subject to pressure which means they can do little more than keep the service going.*
> (Welsh County Authority- Questionnaire response)

The more corporate focus of authorities which has resulted from these changes has in many cases brought libraries into new directorates of leisure amenities or education. There have, however, been some advantages:

> *The library service is now under Libraries, Heritage and Culture which brings a new dimension to the service and opportunities to work with colleagues who have experience of links with arts and cultural organization.*
> (Chief Librarian, London Borough - Questionnaire response)

Even where libraries remain as a department, cross-authority policies for example for under-fives, community care, business or European information or one-stop information shops, have impacted on the priorities for services, whilst the chief officer as a member of a directorate or departmental management team has become increasingly involved with work outside the department. Elected members have become more politicised over this period and involved both in the overall work of the authority and also in individual committees.

2.2.2 Resource allocation and revenue generation

Cuts in public expenditure have in many cases affected libraries disproportionately and chief officers have had to make a very strong case when competing for scarce resources.

Inflation has affected book prices. Over the last decade public library expenditure in the UK has fallen by 12%, whilst book loans have fallen by 19% from 1984/5 to 1994/5. This relates almost totally to adult fiction: adult non-fiction and children's books have held their own.[6,7] Many authorities have responded to changes in the pattern of home based leisure and extended their range of materials to include videos and CDs. They have however usually charged for these additional services. The need for income generation has caused libraries to look to a variety of means of raising income. With the advent of the National Lottery there was hope of Heritage or Millennium funding for libraries but this was initially outside the terms of reference other than extension of buildings for arts activities.[8] However, a number of authorities are currently preparing bids, including a number for reader promotion, in the light of a loosening of these terms. The Arts for everyone initiative is welcomed as an important stimulus to development.[9] The issue of charging in order to meet basic service needs, which was first raised in 1988 in the government's green paper,[10] continues to be a major concern and library services are therefore looking to a wider range of funding, even for core elements of the service such as reading promotion.

2.2.3 Objectives and priorities

In the 1970s, following the Corbett Report - *The libraries' choice*,[11] special services were given a new priority. Community librarianship brought a new emphasis on devising services appropriate to local needs, and community information and business information became important issues. Adult literacy and Open Learning also became new areas for support and information technology became rapidly more important both for housekeeping and for the delivery of information. Beset with new demands from all quarters, the warning of the Library and Information Services Council in 1981 was:

> Since they (public libraries) cannot literally provide the 'comprehensive service' which is asked of them by the Public Libraries and Museums Act 1964 they must in practice select the client groups to whose needs they will give priority in allocating resources.

This was reiterated by the LISC working group on public library objectives who provided an overall mission statement which might be fashioned '*in accordance with existing stock or resource strengths with council policies and with the needs of the community served*'. They also suggested 14 key activities for selection, consistent with the four traditional areas of public library responsibility.

Priority No 13 - recreation - states;

> *The library will develop and publicise its holdings of material in all formats to encourage the creative use of individuals' leisure time. It will assess and respond to the needs of people who use its services in their leisure time, whether for pleasure, information or education. It will recognise in its stock and associated activities that reading is a major form of recreation for many people.*[12]

We were interested to discover how far what had been identified as a key priority was being addressed by libraries, given the need for targeting in the face of resourcing constraints and service demands.

In the questionnaire survey we therefore asked library authorities to express their priority for reading promotion. Ninety-three per cent of libraries rated it as being essential, very important or important.

TABLE 1: *Priority for reading promotion*

Priority	%
Essential	15
Very important	42
Important	36
Not particularly important	6
A waste of resources	-
No answer	1
Total	100

Thirty-one per cent of the authorities responding indicated that they either had a specific statement of aims or objectives regarding reading promotion or that the topic was included in their overall policy statement. Of the 25 authorities who attached copies of their policy documents there were a variety of objectives, including:

> *to promote a love of reading*
> *to encourage awareness of the importance of reading*
> *to provide opportunities for people to experience as wide a range of reading as possible.*
> *to encourage reading for pleasure*
> *to promote a wider use and enjoyment of literature*
> *to offer opportunities for people to satisfy their needs for intellectual development, entertainment, enjoyment and recreation*
> *to seek to promote our stock to library users and the wider public in order to bring as wide a range as possible to the attention of each individual*

We also asked about constraints. Eighty-six per cent of the 122 authorities who responded to this question agreed that there were constraints :

TABLE 2 *Constraints in the promotion on adult reading*

Constraint	%
lack of staff time	41
no specific budget	25
no specific person responsible	16
other*	5
lack of performance measures	3
objectives decided by committee,who do not see this as a priority	1

*also identified were lack of design skills, techniques in encouraging adults to try something new, frequent reorganizations, the nature of the community served and reductions in funding.

One authority wrote that *'constraints only exist as constraints to be overcome'* and another that *'though we are doing all these things the policy isn't yet there'*. Another put into words what may be a more common concern: *'there is the danger of stimulating demand'*.

In other authorities it would appear that the policy for reading promotion is embedded in a book selection policy document. Of the 22 such documents we received, 8 of these included some reference to the promotion of stock in addition to selection and acquisition.

> *'It is recognised that one of the functions of the library service is to promote awareness of the material provided'*

> *'The library will be a prime force in the encouragement of a literary culture through the promotion and enjoyment of reading.'*

> *'It is the function and duty not merely to provide access to a wide range of books but to maximise use by supporting the development of literacy and learning'.*

> `*To promote stock and encourage a wide readership of quality fiction To give the public help in choosing. To increase staff awareness and encourage them to improve their knowledge. To train staff in fiction promotion'.*

> `*To provide but also encourage greatest possible use of stock held'.*

2.2.4 Standards

To translate a policy document into achievable objectives requires a library service to *'ask fundamental questions about what it wants to achieve and how it intends to achieve'*.[13] It will also require a standard against which the objective can be measured.There have been no national standards for England and Wales since the Bourdillon Report.[14] Recently, the Library Association has produced a 'Model statement of standards'[15] 'intended to guide and influence rather than override local standards'. In Scotland, the Convention of Scottish Library Authorities (COSLA) has produced standards[16] which emphasise the need for high quality guiding, presentation, publications and displays and recommend adequate funding and the employment of specialist personnel. These are said to have brought about considerable improvements:

> `The COSLA standards have been endorsed by our council which is very helpful'
> (Scottish library authority questionnaire response)

We found few examples of standards for reading promotion set by local authorities but some examples are:

> 'One county wide reading promotion will be undertaken each year. Both fiction and non fiction will be promoted at all service points. At least 3 lesser known works will be promoted to a wider audience. A minimum of 10,000 booklists will be circulated.'
> (County authority)

> 'Groups will develop a strategy for book stock promotion as part of their annual stock action plan 'Promotional activities will be developed appropriate to local needs and resources...activities envisaged include general or specific book displays, author events and open days' (County authority)

> ... 'a minimum of one planned promotion per librarian per annum' (County authority)

In another authority standards are given; for *'maximum staff participation'*, and *'highest standard of presentation in line with available resources'*.

2.2.5 Service plans

Asking whether there was a specific plan relating to reading promotion we found only 18% of respondents had such a plan. Two authorities indicated a plan was in preparation. We also asked where there was a plan how often it was revised; of the authorities with plans 72% revised their plans annually, 20% every 2-3 years. Nine authorities attached copies of their plans. Examples are:

> 'Areas will provide up to 2 booklists per year.'

> 'Objective-Raise awareness of library stock. Action -Provide bestseller lists in all libraries. 9 booklists. 3 author visits'.

> 'Book clubs and reading groups-Organize reading group programme. Investigate other ways of promotion.'

> 'Our plan will have 14 key activities. Reading and literature will be one of these.'

One authority had a whole-authority approach which included a marketing plan and a staff newsletter to keep up motivation and achieve targets. This resulted from identification to the committee of reading promotion as a key task. In devising policies and service plans a number of authorities had convened working or task groups. One had produced a clear rationale and suggested action in a policy document on reading for pleasure. Overall, though, there appears to be a large gap between what is said to be viewed as a high priority and the realization of that priority through the planning process.

2.2.6 Evaluation

Baker states that *'One step in promotion that is often forgotten (but should not be) is evaluating the results of promotion efforts'.*[17] Overall, there appears to have been little evaluation of adult reading promotion. McKearney, in commenting on the evaluation of Well Worth Reading, deplored the fact that getting feedback from participant libraries was difficult:

> *The length of time it took to get the information was instructive and led us to the conclusion that libraries are, in some important respects, not very tuned into the evaluative aspects of marketing and the needs of the market place (i.e., having the information to convince potential funding partners that they are worth investing in).*[18]

Where schemes are funded by regional arts or the Arts Council this is part of the project, and may be one of the most useful aspects of libraries' association with arts marketing bodies. In the Library Fund promotions written up in Shelf Talk[19] evaluation is a key part of each project. For instance, in 'The Novel Takeaway' organized by Berkshire, *'evaluation was regarded as a central part of the project. It is important that librarians know how effective particular types of promotion are'.* One authority which has prioritized display as its main means of promotion has used control libraries, issues and user reactions to evaluate its policy. We found further examples in our study, but the pattern overall was similar to that in other studies: some evidence of good practice, but a lack of consistent application of evaluation.

The London Borough of Bromley, which has developed along the lines of alternative arrangements, was asked to produce a report on a pilot scheme for its committee. This is a detailed evaluation of the development.

Birmingham conducted a major consultation exercise on fiction and discovered that:

> *'users would welcome any initiative which would assist them in making their choice. A number of those interviewed made use of reviews in newspapers or magazines to inform their reading. It was also evident that expectations had been raised by the sophisticated marketing techniques of large bookstores. In particular, readers would*

*like book review and literary magazines, staff recommendations, information about
authors, book displays, more visual impact e.g., paperbacks displayed front facing.*

2.2.7 User studies

One of the effects of government legislation has been the development
by individual authorities of user studies, causing them to investigate user
satisfaction and analyze use as part of their overall evaluation of services.
In line with the Citizen's Charter it is necessary to consult the public on
needs and their satisfaction through service provision. Asked about user
surveys, only 17% of library services had conducted studies into how
readers choose their books; 10% of authorities had undertaken studies
into evaluation of methods of adult reading promotion and 8% had
looked into book selection related to reading promotion. The majority of
library studies have been fairly broad brush in regard to analysis of
reading needs or reading promotion. User surveys have largely been
undertaken to a *pro forma* devised by CIPFA/Audit Commission which
includes questions on a 'needs fill basis' i.e., have users found what they
want. Readers are asked if they were seeking specific authors, titles or
subjects, if they were successful and if they came into the library with a
particular book in mind did they obtain it. It would appear the reader is
seldom asked why they chose a particular book and whether they
enjoyed it or how effectively they are helped to find the book they want.
Hatt argues that these kinds of question are more to do with reader
behaviour than reader needs.[20]

TABLE 3: *User studies*

User studies	%
How readers choose their books	17
Evaluation of methods of reading promotion	10
Book selection related to reading promotion	8

2.2.8 Performance indicators

The government's requirement for libraries to show value for money and
justify their existence has focused attention on performance indicators.
The Audit Commission requirement for England and Wales is quite
limited: information on number of users, number of visits, opening hours
and costs per capita on a two year comparison[21] while Scotland has an
added indicator on staff costs per issue. A value for money study on
libraries is currently being undertaken which is likely to develop further
performance indicators in due course.[22] Although *Keys to success:*

performance indicators for public libraries was produced to help library services in designing such measures it has had limited impact on the kinds of measurement being undertaken. Measurement must be related to the particular objectives of the organization and instances are given in *Keys to success* of particular indicators that might be used, for book discussion groups, children's story hours and so on. It is left to the authority to ascribe activities to a particular objective. The measures are both quantitative e.g., number of activities held, people attending, and qualitative: user satisfaction with frequency, user satisfaction with event, etc. Quality is measured by 'expert rating to a standard' and again this is left to be devised locally.[23] However, despite the availability of this advice, we found problems in the development of appropriate indicators to measure quality of book provision and reader satisfaction.

> *There is difficulty in devising performance indicators. Satisfaction with the range of stock is fairly simple but satisfaction with the book (selected by or suggested to the reader) is more difficult.*

> *The development of a wider range of performance indicators against which performance will be monitored in future remains an imperative if a fuller picture is to be gained* (Chief Librarian of Municipal Library and Information service)

Of the returns, 16% of the authorities used some sort of performance measures for reading promotion, e.g.,

> *'to plan 30 stock promotions a year'*
> *'minimising the quantity of dead stock related to the promotion of that stock area.'*
> *'Comparison of issues over the same books in other libraries'*
> *'Customer reservations and Customer comments'*
> *'Use of the stock promoted'*
> *'Number of promotional activities by type'*

It would appear that the development of performance indicators for reading promotion is still at an early stage and at present not related to overall objectives and strategies.

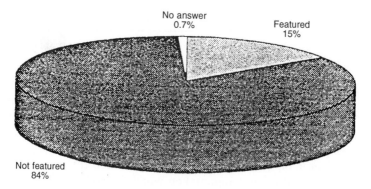

FIG. 1: *Performance indicators for reading promotion*

2.2.9 The citizen's charter

The appropriate response to user studies is some form of action, either to explain to users why it is not feasible to satisfy their demands or to develop the service to meet their needs, following on from the Citizen's Charter initiative.[24] Promises in line with the Charter for Public Libraries[25] are indicated in some of the policy documents which were sent to us, but often to do with stock rather than promotion:

> 'Our range of stock will cover the educational, cultural, information and leisure interests of the community'
>
> 'We will buy enough copies of the most important works of modern English fiction and poetry.'
>
> 'The range and depth of our non fiction stocks will meet the needs of the local community'.

And one which is specifically related to fiction:

> 'Through their local library the customers of [x county] libraries have the right to expect access to:-
>
> A broad range of general fiction ; classics and set tests; special interest fiction; the current best sellers; a representative selection of first novels; fiction written in a foreign language; a broad and frequently changed stock of poetry; a broad range of fiction in large print and on tape; staff with specialist knowledge of fiction book news and information; in addition they also have the right to expect libraries where books are arranged to enable ease of use and selection; fiction displays as appropriate; books in good physical condition'.

And one on finding materials:

> 'We will help you find stock by providing guides, catalogues and a readers advisory service.'

However, these appear to be the exceptions. We received few indications of promises on stock or promotion in line with the Citizen's Charter.

2.2.10 Staffing in public libraries

In the early '70s, many library services were subjected to a review of the staffing structures by their authorities' organization and methods teams. This, and an increasingly tight financial climate, caused the majority of services to begin more clearly to define 'professional' and 'non-professional' duties. The use of library assistants to staff smaller or more rural libraries is nothing new but the more scientific analysis of responsibilities brought in new hierarchies of the non-professional staff as 'library managers' responsible for the day to day up-keep of the library and teams of peripatetic librarians who were given responsibility usually for stock, for scheduled cover of enquiry desks and for making community contacts. In larger libraries, librarians and support staff have therefore been working more closely together and there are perhaps clearer lines of responsibility. We found that this was a common pattern for our respondents.

> 'Not all libraries have professional staff. It's a parallel structure - professional and non-professional. The non-professionals we rely on to manage libraries, to run the operation, to run a tight ship. The emphasis is on customer service people skills ensuring tidyness and presentation. Nowhere is it explicit in the job description that they answer queries. Librarians are not line managers and they have to rely on a strong steer which hopefully library managers will accept.

> In recruitment of library managers and their staffs, management are usually placing an emphasis on good organizational skills and 'customer care' qualities but not necessarily looking for people who were readers themselves or who knew about books. You can't put it in the recruitment policy that we only employ people who enjoy reading.' (Team leader, County authority - Telephone Interview)

Another authority admitted that they did not question potential applicants about books :

> 'I suppose we have a stereotype of people who are readers not being people -related or efficient.'
> (Senior Librarian, County authority - Telephone Interview)

> 'Looking for staff with book knowledge has rather disappeared - it's no longer essential but desirable. It's a people service now more that than about reading, nor is it about IT; staff are there as intermediaries'.
> (Chief Librarian, London Borough.)

> 'Recruitment hasn't always required book knowledge or interpersonal skills as criteria.'
> (County Librarian- Telephone Interview)

Enquiry handling is often 'networked' to larger libraries or it is suggested to the public that they ask for help at times when the enquiry desk would be manned by a librarian. The emphasis on information has in many cases changed the 'enquiry desk' to 'information service' and whilst book lending enquiries are still handled there, any of the reader contacts for registration, requests or purely directional enquiries are dealt with by counter staff.

The organization of staffing has a clear bearing on the promotion of reading to adults. One factor which has emerged is the variation and sometimes uncertainty of where reading promotion comes in the overall responsibilities of management. This has an effect on staff enthusiasm and motivation:

> 'Many staff are keen but without priority given at the top, and a block on certain promotion methods. It is very frustrating'
> (Senior Librarian, Metropolitan Borough - Questionnaire response.)

2.2.11 Management

In answer to the question 'Within your library service management team is there a post with overall responsibility for reading promotion?' only 30% of respondents could identify such a post.

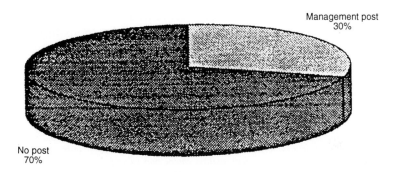

FIG. 2: *Management responsibility for reading promotion*

In many authorities there is an advisory post with responsibilities for special aspects of the service, including work with children, information, music or local studies. Seeking to establish whether there were similar posts for reading promotion brought a positive response from 24% of authorities who had such a post - usually combined with other duties.

Sometimes the responsibility is with the head of Bibliographical Services but there the emphasis was usually on stock selection and acquisition. In one authority the stock and promotion librarian is responsible to a County Bibliographical Services officer. Duties include

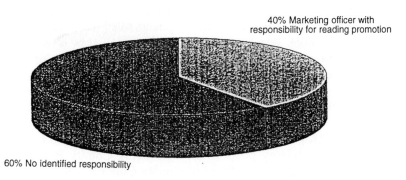

FIG. 3: *Advisory posts for reading promotion*

> *'identifying and developing opportunities for the promotion and exploitation of the County stock including the management of the exhibitions service.'*

In another authority, reading promotion is seen as part of an overall stock responsibility and the post-holder is expected to *'develop county wide programmes which aim to promote reading for information and leisure.'*

In the survey, we found some evidence of restructuring to provide posts with a lead role in reader services; it would also appear that some authorities are seeking to change the balance of responsibilities with more priority on promotion.

Leeds has recently advertised for a Head of Reader Services with the task of leading both stock management and literature development. The post is identified as part of the policy forum for the service. The duties are:

> *to formulate, monitor and co-ordinate the delivery of reader development and stock management strategies; to co-ordinate the work of group librarians in terms of reader development, ensuring consistent quality, choice and value for money; to lead on literature development initiatives and partnerships'.*
>
> (Leeds Library and Information Service)

They have also established a second post of literature development advisor which is to be

> *'accountable for co-ordinating literature based events and activities across the city; for developing staff knowledge of books and reading; [and] plan and co-ordinate city wide literature events such as festivals ; initiate reading groups;monitoring standards and developments leading to increased use and discovery by current and potential library users'.*

Oxfordshire has restructured its service to develop reading and readers. Describing it as a process which is in progress, we found that this started with a library collections management review to identify the 'core activities of librarians'. These were identified as reader services, stock management and a community development role. By cutting down the time spent on book selection which is now controlled by a small team of 'experts,' it has been possible to devote more time to Reader Services, including promotion. According to the County Literature Librarian this has greatly benefited the service and widened its client base. The change, which has been facilitated by external consultants, has developed the advisory role of librarians, but the emphasis has been on indirect advice through promotion. The post of County Literature Librarian is one of three advisory posts (the others being County Reference and Information Librarian and Head of County Children's Services) with a county-wide advisory role for stock management and promotion. In each of the three areas the senior librarian (reader services) who works to an assistant county librarian, is responsible for the teams of clerical and professional staff in their area.

In Bexley, we found a similar stress placed on stock selection, with the service specification for the branch library network stating:

> *Bexley library services places a high value on the bibliographical knowledge and stock selection skills of professional staff. All members of the professional staff are expected to read widely so as to be able to recommend interesting books to users. Staff are encouraged to keep themselves up to date with new publications, to be aware of those books which are awarded literary prizes, to follow developments in the book trade and to understand popular tastes in reading materials. Professional library managers are expected to be skilled bookpeople.*
>
> (Bexley Education and Leisure Services Directorate - specification revised 1997.)

The link between marketing and the promotion of reading was also examined as part of our investigation of the management of reading promotion. While 26% of authorities had a marketing officer, reading promotion was considered to be part of their duties in only 40% of these. That the concept of promotion of a core service area should be so rarely related to other marketing activities gives rise for concern, but endorses previous studies of library services marketing, in which a similarly low level of strategic marketing was discovered.[26] (This relationship is examined further in chapter 5.)

To ascertain the quality of advice given on reading, the question was asked: Do any of your libraries have a post of Readers Advisor? Only 10% of the respondents identified such a post, a role which we examine

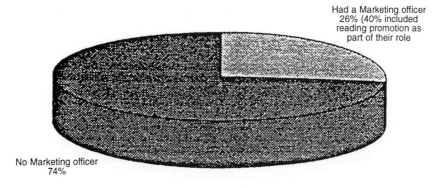

FIG. 4: *Libraries with marketing officers with responsibility for reading promotion*

in more detail in chapter 4. In a number of authorities the post of literature development worker, usually not a professional librarian and normally of short term duration, had provided the inspiration and the co-ordination for reading promotion. The danger here is isolation and the possibility that reading becomes seen as 'their' role and not as part of the core business of the library service.

2.2.12 Budget

We asked if there was a specific budget for reading promotion and for a broad indication of sums allocated. While this is always a difficult issue when so many budgets for promotion and marketing are aggregated with other budget heads, the sums indicated were nevertheless disappointing. Clearly the very small amounts of money which are invested in book promotion compare unfavourably with the immense sums in the book trade. One authority, which 'earmarked' money in 1996 and achieved a very successful promotion, feels that in the light of its reduced total budget it can no longer do so. Another authority is deliberately spending more on staff and promotions and less on books and gaining increased issues that way.

At a very conservative estimate it would appear that libraries are spending c £200,000 on promotion compared with £1.7 billion spent in 1996/7 by bookshops. Reasons for this very cautious approach to spending on promotion need to be investigated, particularly in the light of advice which suggests the need to promote whole library stocks at times of reduced spending.

2.2.13 Book suppliers and reading promotion

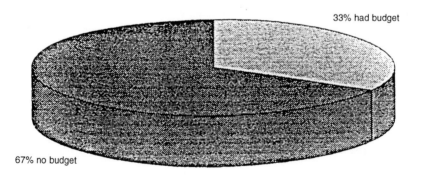

33% had budget

67% no budget

FIGS. 5: *Budgets for reading promotion*

Book-supply procedures are also changing. The traditional relationship

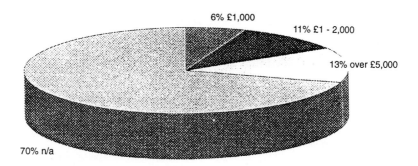

6% £1,000

11% £1 - 2,000

13% over £5,000

70% n/a

FIGS. 6: *Budgets for reading promotion*

between library suppliers and library authorities, built up over the years, has been understanding and supportive. Library suppliers have endeavoured to encourage librarians to However the threat of CCT and more recently the EC rulings concerning tendering have changed the relationship to a more business-like tendering process:[27,28]

> *'We will establish trading relationships with a range of suppliers'. 'We will assess the suitability of individual suppliers by means of an agreement.'*
> (Library Book Selection Policy document)

The ending of the Net Book Agreement (NBA) has taken this a step further, with library authorities now seeking to get the best discount possible and in some cases value-added support as well. A number of library authorities expressed their reliance on suppliers to fund reading promotion initiative programmes. This added value can take many forms: display materials, dump-bins, printed publicity or author visits.

Where libraries are working together in consortia, there are hopes that combined buying power gives 'muscle'. With the end of the NBA causing suppliers to look for ways of reducing overheads, it is suggested that suppliers may also benefit from these promotions by using materials which they would have once designed themselves and by exploiting the marketing opportunity.

> *'We are giving the supplier information and they are using this to stock extra sets to sell to other libraries; it's a win/win situation, it makes what we are doing sustainable '.*
> (Municiple authority - telephone interview)

On the other hand some suppliers are taking a more guarded line:

> *'Library suppliers are ideally placed to suggest promotions but with the NBA issue the soft things round the edges have had to go. It's now a more business -like negotiation and the spirit of partnership is more difficult. In tendering, the calculation*

of discount is clinical. There is no spare capacity to support library promotions - the non-core business is no longer realistic, it is possible for suppliers to agree to benefit in kind instead of discount but libraries must choose, they can't have it both ways'
(Manager, library supplier - Personal Interview)

Another supplier stated that it is: `

only possible to give a measured discount from a menu of services including promotion. Libraries should not expect to get maximum discount and additional services. This is equally true where libraries work in consortia with combined spending power and suppliers who are providing maximum discount and additional services will not survive. Unless libraries are realistic, there is a strong danger of losing promotional support.
(Manager, library supplier - telephone interview.)

We asked library authorities if they had been involved with any joint initiatives with library suppliers in the previous year; 29% of them had organised activities with the support of a supplier. With library book funds continually under pressure, authorities may have to decide, if they want to develop reading promotion, whether to continue to use the suppliers with their network of contacts and marketing experience, and accept less discount or to set aside their own specific budget.

2.2.14 Book selection policies

We sought to establish what was the trend in terms of book selection policies. With decreasing book funds, falling issues and the demands which are encouraged by the ideals of Citizen's Charter and user surveys, were libraries taking a more demand-driven approach to stock purchasing or did they still see their role as custodians of our literary heritage, encouraging a literate society? As Usherwood argues:

'At some point the public library will have to be faced with the central dichotomy of value versus demand. Basically do you give the public what they want or do you concentrate on materials considered good?'[29]

The answer had obvious implications for this study of reading promotion.We asked libraries to state their <u>main</u> aim in book selection, giving them a choice of five descriptors - or if they preferred their own short descriptor:

A quarter of the authorities were unable to prioritise any of the suggested criteria since their policies reflected all factors equally. '

I felt it would be misleading to choose only from these as most libraries are fundamentally concerned with striking a balance'.

TABLE 4: *Book selection policies*

MAIN AIM	%
to cater for all tastes	49
other/all aims important/own document	11
emphasis is given to new titles likely to be in demand	10
we look for books which will complement existing collections	7
referral to mission/policy statement	5
broad range of materials/appropriate use/quality material/within restricted budget	5
we ensure that selection includes important titles which might not fit the stereotype of the average reader	5
to satisfy customer/local community needs	4
emphasis is given to new titles to be in demand	4

We received 23 book selection policies, which were analyzed to identify common issues and interesting examples. Aims included the following:

> 'To cater for actual and potential users' needs'.

> 'There should be acceptable levels of work by literary authors, standard and modern'.

> 'Ephemeral fiction should be provided to encourage all to read but not at the expense of more serious stock'.

> 'We will not purchase a disproportionate amount of ephemeral fiction at the expense of more serious works'

> 'We consider it important not to stereotype a community or distort the balance'

> 'It is important not to distort the balance of stock in response to readers' demands'.

> 'To cater for all tastes, but Central has a positive commitment to quality at the expense of high issues'

It would appear, though, that there may be a gap between these broad philosophical statements with the laudable aims of widening stock provision and encouraging more adventurous reading by users and the practicality of selection. Community librarianship has encouraged the concept that only the local librarian knows the local community sufficiently well to select stock for them, but at the same time there seems to be a cautious attitude on the part of librarians when selecting for their users. Concern is now being expressed at the consequent preponderance of high-issuing, popular material:

> 'The tendency to devolve stock selection has in practice meant that a great deal of time has gone into the process but in effect the stock selected has tended to be the same.'
>
> (County literature librarian.)

Van Riel criticises librarians for selecting 'safe' issue fodder.

> There is this terrible pull of middle of the roadism. People are afraid to make a recommendation that is going to move people from the very safe area. They're afraid

> *that someone will complain or they'll be held personally responsible. And that is because there is no clear policy within the authority for this area of activity.*[30]

The County Librarian of Oxfordshire has also addressed this problem and is quoted as saying that

> *'unless authorities revise their selection policies, the range of titles will narrow'.*

In his authority,

> *'Library managers were involved but we've changed that, the next step is to change the balance of librarians, from everyone being involved in selection to using that time for promotion.'*

The Director of the Library and Information Statistics Unit (LISU) similarly comments that:

> *Libraries have a terrific influence on the publishing of first and second novels and this is an area which needs more care and attention from librarians. After all, the novelists that survive their early days and go into paperback, become the Graham Greenes of later years'.*

`Fringe benefits' is an Arts Council-funded project which aims to develop an objective vocabulary for describing and evaluating literature under-represented in public libraries. Operating in Buckinghamshire, Berkshire and Oxfordshire, it will seek to define how books can be objectively evaluated without actually reading them.[31] The intention is to encourage wider dissemination of less read material.

Book selection processes are becoming more streamlined in some authorities. There is a number of reasons for this; the decrease in bookfunds, the new contracts with suppliers, a more structured approach to stock buying with use of management information and the 'tiering 'of libraries (a means of calculating quantity and type of stock according to size). Several authorities indicated that they were now putting libraries into tiers or bands.

> *'tiering provides an effective framework under which planning development and resource distribution can take place. It enables the achievement of quality and consistency of service delivery and gives a sound basis for the monitoring of performance and increased accountability to users.'*
>
> (Selection Policy document, County authority)

In asking about the selection process we were particularly interested to see whether the use of CD-ROMs as a selection tool had any bearing on the way books were selected and consequently on the promotion of resources. Forty-seven per cent of libraries are now using CD-ROMs as a selection tool; 83 % still use approval collections, with several of our sample using both of these methods and 51% using a range of methods which may include local bookshops and book lists. One supplier indicated that currently one-third of their customers select from a CD-

ROM. In this case selectors can choose to view by topic or by level; they can see a book's cover, back cover or blurb, a spread of inside pages, contents/index and orders can be placed in a variety of ways. This supplier outlined the advantages and disadvantages:

> *'It saves supply time and keeps down costs, saves librarian time handling books, it's easily portable, it's more structured as a selection tool than handling the books, it's flexible and encourages lateral thinking. It has potential use for the public. The disadvantages: some libraries haven't yet got the technology, but more importantly this is an issue for the profession regarding the role of the librarian - in some ways it hits at the heart of the profession'.*

One Assistant County Librarian stated that it was much easier to hold an effective book selection meeting with CD-ROMs; previously librarians looked at books in isolation while now they discussed them objectively. Blanshard, writing about book selection for children, agrees that use of CD-ROMs will save time which can be redirected to the front line.[32]

There are many other issues which are currently on the agenda in relation to materials selection: the stocking of audio visual materials and their relationship to books, polices for equal opportunities, etc, but the issue of specific interest for this survey was highlighted by one County Librarian;

> *'Librarians must spend less time on selection and more on promotion if we are going to make any headway at all'.*

We found that selection was a key area and that there is a need for more information on how libraries are selecting and buying their books, given the significance of an activity which lies at the root of professional librarians' roles in serving communities' needs.

2.2.15 Future developments

Finally, we asked authorities to tell us what further development they might see in the foreseeable future . There were some encouraging signs:

> *'This is a new authority, my aim is to put promotion, including reading promotion at the top of the agenda.'*
> (County Librarian Scottish Authority- questionnaire response)

> *'There is in this authority a huge change of emphasis towards reading promotion.'*
> (Senior Librarian London Borough - questionnaire response)

> *'Attitudes are changing and staff are beginning to see the importance of reading. we have the foundation stone firmly laid and now need to start building.'*
> (Assistant Director - County service- questionnaire response)

> *... 'the previous authority appeared to believe that acquisition is sufficient. We believe that exploitation is critical to future success.'*
> (Chief Librarian, metropolitan district - questionnaire response)

'Reading development should become a more developed part of the service in future years, a higher profile, better marketing, better displays.'
(Senior Librarian, metropolitan district - questionnaire response).

But one authority warns

'There is a need to grow to stand still or the motivation will drop back'
(Senior Librarian, metropolitan district - questionnaire response)

2.3. Summary

Despite the difficulties facing public libraries at present, difficulties which include lack of resourcing, political turbulence and restructuring, there is evidence of considerable concern to develop reading promotion and a recognition that this is a core activity. We found, though, that the extent to which this is promulgated through action planning was limited. Some concern was also felt at the low levels of funding dedicated specifically to reading promotion. It was also seen that book selection practices required further investigation and consideration, and that this major professional task needed to be better balanced with promotional work.

References

1. COXALL, B. *and* L. ROBINS. *Contemporary British politics.* London: Macmillan, 1994.

2. KELLY, T. *History of public libraries in Great Britain.* 2nd ed. London: Library Association, 1977, 435.

3. *The conduct of local authority business.* (The Widdicombe Report) London: HMSO, 1986.

4. KPMG AND CAPITAL PLANNING INFORMATION. *Contracting out in public libraries.* London: KPMG, 1995.

5. DEPARTMENT OF NATIONAL HERITAGE. News release. December 18, 1995.

6. NATIONAL BOOK COMMITTEE. *Public libraries and their book funds.* London: Book Trust, 1997.

7. *Ibid.,* 5.

8. *Cultural Trends no 24. Books, libraries and reading.* London: Policy Studies Institute, 1994.

9. ARTS COUNCIL OF ENGLAND. *Arts 4 everyone.* London: Arts Council, 1997.

10. OFFICE OF ARTS AND LIBRARIES. *Financing our public library service.* London: HMSO, 1988.

11. DEPARTMENT OF EDUCATION AND SCIENCE. *The libraries' choice.* (The Corbett Report) London: HMSO, 1978.

12. LIBRARY AND INFORMATION SERVICES COUNCIL WORKING GROUP ON PUBLIC LIBRARY OBJECTIVES. *Setting objectives for public library services.* London: HMSO, 1991.

13. *Ibid.,* 17.

14. MINISTRY OF EDUCATION. *Standards of public library service in England and Wales.* (The Bourdillon Report) London: HMSO, 1962.

15. LIBRARY ASSOCIATION. *Model statement of standards.* London: Library Association, 1994.

16. CONVENTION OF SCOTTISH LIBRARY AUTHORITIES. *Standards for the public library service in Scotland.* Edinburgh: COSLA, 1986.

17. BAKER, S. L. *The responsive public library collection.* Colorado: Libraries Unlimited, 1993, 161.

18. MCKEARNEY, M. Well worth reading: fiction promotion scheme comes of age. *Public Libraries Journal ,* 5 (3), 62.

19. STEWART, I. *Shelf talk: promoting literature in public libraries.* London: The Arts Council for England, The Library Association, 1996.

20. HATT, F. *The reading process: a framework for analysis and description.* London: Bingley, 1976.

21. AUDIT COMMISSION FOR LOCAL GOVERNMENT IN ENGLAND AND WALES. *Performance review in local government: leisure and libraries.* London: HMSO, 1986.

22. KENNEDY, J. Looking at value for money. *Library Association Record,* 99(1) January, 1997 32-33

23. KING RESEARCH. *Keys to success: a manual of performance indicators for UK public libraries.* London: HMSO, 1990.

24. *The Citizen's charter.* London: HMSO,1991.

25. LIBRARY ASSOCIATION. *A charter for public libraries.* London: The Library Association, 1993.

26. KINNELL, M. *and* J. MACDOUGALL. *Meeting the marketing challenge: strategies for public libraries and leisure services.* London: Taylor Graham, 1994, 63-78.

27. EUROPEAN COMMISSION. Supplies directive 93/36/EC. Brussels: EC, 1993.

28. EUROPEAN COMMISSION. Services directive 92/50/EC. Brussels: EC, 1992.

29. USHERWOOD, R. *Rediscovering public library management.* London: Library Association Publishing, 1996.

30. VAN RIEL, R. In: Watson, D. Impowering literary choice. *Library Association Record,* 98(9), 1996, 463.

31. Literature news. Fringe project starts. *Library Association Record,* 99 (3), 1997, 132.

32. BLANSHARD, C. The electronic approval system. *Library Association Record,* 99(1), 1997.

3. Reading literature and the book world

In this chapter we review the evidence for the status of reading in today's society, and responses of the arts bodies and booksellers which have relevance for libraries. Relationships with the book trade are of fundamental importance to libraries' success in meeting their readers' aspirations for wide-ranging provision of all kinds of material. There are also lessons that can be learned from effective commercial promotion and merchandising techniques, and from targeted staff training.

3.1 Reading as a pastime

Despite all the other forms of leisure pursuits which are available, reading is still a popular pastime, as is shown in the table below, which describes popular trends over a three-year period, from a wide-ranging study of leisure activities.[1]

Bookmarketing Ltd, an independent book research and information body which took over the marketing role of the Publisher's Association in 1990, has also undertaken research which identifies how far popular reading remains a significant aspect of leisure activity. Their ongoing research into books and the consumer is based on a panel of 8000 nationally representative households, with the 1995 survey showing that just under half the population claimed to be reading a book for pleasure at the time of interview. Given a margin for error, the percentages remained remarkably constant over a seven-year period.[2]

Sixty-three per cent of adults read books for general interest and 54% to gain information, while as many as 74% had 'read at all' in the four weeks prior to interview. Thirty per cent of those interviewed had finished a book approximately one week previously; 55% of women and 40% of men read 'regularly' and 21% of women and 26% of men read occasionally. Social groups A and B read most - 67% being regular readers - against 57% of C1; 40 % of C D; and 39% of D E. From the viewpoint of both the book trade and of libraries, reasons that are given for not reading are as important as these encouraging statistics for leisure reading. In the report of the 1995 survey, it was interesting to note that most of the reasons involved choice over the allocation of time and motivation to read rather than physical difficultes such as poor sight, or low educational attainment as reflected in an individual's inability to read. Simply having time in a busy schedule was the major constraint. Interestingly, while the figures for leisure reading had remained steady between 1989 and 1995 the reasons for *not* reading did shift, reflecting changes in working lives during this period. Longer working hours have had a measurable impact on individuals' ability to choose reading amongst a range of leisure options.[3]

TABLE 5 : *Reading and other leisure interests*

	1993 %	1994 %	1995 %
Watching TV	97	97	98
Reading newspapers	82	79	81
Listening to the radio	-	73	76
Reading books	60	59	62
Listening to CDs tapes etc.	58	59	60
Drinking alcohol at home	52	57	56
Watching videos recorded	47	47	49
Gardening	50	45	47
Caring for pets	44	41	43
Playing with children	42	44	42
Reading general magazines	37	38	42
Reading special interest magazines	37	39	40
Cooking for pleasure	37	37	40
Watching other videos	27	29	32
Sewing/knitting	20	20	21
Exercising at home	18	19	17
Using home computer	9	12	15
Playing games on computer console	11	10	10

TABLE 6: *Percentage of population as leisure readers*

1989	1990	1991	1992	1993	1994	1995
45	47	46	45	51	51	48

TABLE 7: *Non-readers' reasons for not reading*

	1989	1995
No time/not enough time/too much work/long hours	33	44
Don't enjoy it/doesn't interest me	21	24
Enough to do already/occupied with/prefer other things	46	27
Only read magazines/newspapers	9	10
Find it difficult/not very good reader	5	2
Bad eyesight/hurts my eyes	5	6
Other answers/don't know	13	19

Predictably, reading patterns vary across the age ranges, with time spent reading for pleasure averaging just over 7 hours a week. In 1993, the 65+ age group spent nearly twice as much time reading (10.4 hours per week) as the 15-24 age group (5.6 hours per week).[4] The types of books read indicated gender differences, but with little variation between 1989 and 1993 in overall reading figures other than a marked decline in romance/love fiction reading and some fall-off in preference for short stories and travel books.[5]

While these findings relate to statistics from some years ago, confirmation that reading as a leisure activity continues to hold up comes from a recent investigation by the Policy Studies Institute. This revealed that people are reading more and watching less television despite the launch of cable and satellite channels. One in five people said they had read a novel for pleasure in the last week.[6]

TABLE 8: *Types of books read*

FICTION		1989	1993		
	All %	Men %	Women %	All %	
Crime/thriller/detective	37	32	36	34	
Romance/love	31	3	43	24	
Historical novel/romance	28	17	31	24	
War/adventure	26	28	13	20	
Short stories	24	13	21	17	
Science fiction/fantasy	16	23	9	16	
20th Century	18	12	17	15	
Humour/cartoon	21	17	10	14	
Books based on TV/films	18	10	17	14	
Horror/occult	14	13	13	13	
Classics/literature	14	13	15	13	
Any fiction	75	66	78	72	
NON FICTION					
Puzzle/Quiz	20	16	27	22	
True life	20	18	22	20	
Biography/autobiography	19	14	23	19	
Food/drink	20	13	25	19	
Nature/wildlife	14	22	25	17	
History	18	15	13	17	
Travel	21	17	19	16	
Sports/games	16	24	6	14	
War	10	19	3	11	
Antiques/collecting	9	10	10	10	
Any Non Fiction	74	76	77	76	

3.2 Research on reading

As we can see from the above studies, there is now a reasonable amount of factual data on the numbers of people who read, how they obtain their books and in broad terms their book interests. There is also no shortage of writing about the pleasure of reading from a personal and subjective perspective, but there is a lack of sociological data of a systematic nature on the role of books in society and the part they play in people's lives.[7] As Manguel has shown, the relationship between social structures and the act of reading is a complex one: the privacy we associate now with leisure reading came relatively late to Western society, which affected the space for reading. And the relationship between reader and writer is open to endless speculation.[8] Mann and Burgoyne found that the bulk of British research into book reading had been largely along the lines of simple market surveys[9] and in *From author to reader* it is noted that whilst the value of reading good books is constantly asserted there is little evidence to back this up.[10] This lack of research is also noted by Hatt who argues that attention has been focused on teaching the basic skills of reading at the one end and the mechanistic process of 'quicker reading 'at the other whilst giving scant regard to the reader's *'purpose, response, reaction and evaluation'.*[11]

Karetsky states that research into the sociological aspects of reading stems from the disciplines of education, literature, sociology and librarianship. It is *'international and interdisciplinary but its centre was with American librarianship...its most productive decade 1929 - 39'.* In his analysis, Karetsky surmises that the limitations of the literature promotion movement and its research resulted from the uncertainties about the place of librarianship as a profession at that time: an interesting parallel with the present situation.[12] While Gray and Monroe summarised studies of adult reading in America between 1900 and 1928[13] it was Douglas Waples who became the leader in this field, through his introduction of social science methods into the study of reading. One of his main conclusions was that whilst people said they liked to read about *'matters of real importance'*, in effect people like to read about themselves. The more closely a subject relates to the familiar the more interesting it is to the reader.[14]

A Russian librarian, Nicholas Rubakin, had earlier developed a science of the psychology of reading, 'bibliopsychology', with a twenty-nine year research project which began in 1889 . His international questionnaire 'Reader know thyself' sought to analyze data on the respondents, their emotional responses and thought processes when reading a specific book.[15] According to Simsova, only Poland now shows an interest in the work of Rubakin because there the study of reading is given some prominence. She argues that the value of bibliopsychology lies in the insight given to the interaction between book and reader.[16] Arguably, if these principles were to be applied today there could be more satisfied readers through books being more effectively targeted at specific groups. *Opening the book: finding a good read*, attempts to achieve just this.[17]

In Britain reading research became to some extent subsumed in *'debates over whether libraries should give the public what it wants or what it the library thinks it should want'*[18] and although the need for research was advocated by figures such as Sayers[19] and Munford[20] the major concern was the 'fiction question' and not much research on reading was actually undertaken. Peter Mann produced a 'sociological model' for reading which was based on a continuum of work - leisure, but argued that although a specialist monograph may not be intended for light reading or a thriller for scholarly analysis, the reader may choose to perceive it in this way.[21] We therefore still know little about the motives for reading and why, for instance, people read serious modern fiction - although there have been various attempts to explain this.

Brewis, Geriche and Kruger give a variety of reasons for the reading of fiction; reading to relieve tension, to enhance societal consciousness, for clarification of personal or social values, for escape, for knowledge, to solve personal problems and reading for pleasure (amusement, entertainment and relaxation).[22]

According to McClellan there are deeper psychological reasons including empathy, extending understanding, to gain a sense of belonging, to help defuse feelings, to confirm our beliefs, to find meaning, to test out theories or plans, or to give space or equilibrium thus allowing the unconscious to absorb or deal with difficulties or problems. McClellan states that:

> *'the prediction of responses by a number of unknown potential readers is virtually impossible and furthermore we cannot therefore with any certainty assess the kinds of values which actually emerge from the reading of a particular text'.*

Research into reading is therefore self-limiting by the very nature of the act of reading.[23]

In an attempt to move on from this position and to categorize and define reading Nell refers to two types: 'work reading' and 'lucid' or pleasure reading. He identifies that the 'lucid' reader can gain more pleasure than by watching TV or going to the theatre and also may get deep relaxation and *'most startling changes of mood'*.[24] Wiegard found that stabilisation of the individual's personal life is the greatest gain[25] whereas Zaaiman's view was that the emotional and intellectual experiences of light fiction readers were no less valid than those gained from reading literary fiction - a factor that public libraries should now acknowledge.[26]

Luckham considers that constancy is the major feature of reading and notes that the ordinary citizen is *'stable and determined in his [sic] tastes and institutional manipulation and moulding can be successfully resisted'*.[27] He notes that changes in society are reflected in reading and acknowledges the difficulty of research in this field both in terms of expense and intrusiveness and suggests the need for personal longitudinal studies looking perhaps at changes at different stages of life, such as the teenage years, retirement, etc.

In *Borrowed time*, attention is drawn to reading for informal learning, questioning whether education and leisure are incompatible philosophies: *'the best of leisure and the best of education are one and the same thing'* and reading for information and self improvement and empowerment is a justifiable use of leisure time.[28]

O'Rourke also warns against judging readers by their reading material:

> *'...how little we know of the nature and significance of reading'* and maintains that *'the arguments that reading genre fiction , especially if it is read exclusively, limitspeople's knowledge, moral outlook and language skills. The argument and its obverse that reading ... is an enriching and improving experience is not proven.*[29]

Sabine and Sabine interviewed 1382 American people to find what book made the greatest difference in their lives and while the results are anecdotal they provide further insight into areas which are difficult to probe using scientific research methods.[30] Ethnographic and other qualitative methodologies which delve further into motivation and impact are likely to offer richer data and provide more answers to the questions which librarians and others involved in promoting books are asking about why people read and what motivates them. This approach is exemplified in a study by Hamshere, who examined the needs fulfilled by borrowing books from a public library. She combines in her qualitative study, the 'uses and gratifications' approach of mass media studies, i.e., what users expect to get out of reading and what 'gratification' they receive, and the 'reader response' theory of literary criticism which places the reader in an active role as 'co-creator' of the text, *'guided by the text but also influenced by what the reader brings to the reading in terms of their own experience thoughts and beliefs'*.[31]

3.3 Literature, reading promotion and the Arts Council

Against this background of only partially answered questions about what people are reading and why, there has nevertheless been some attempt to co-ordinate the promotion of literature as one of the elements in a national policy for the arts. The Arts Council of Great Britain was formed in 1946 to support and develop the performing arts and in 1994 separate councils were established for Scotland and Wales. Northern Ireland had its own separate Council from the start, while in England it was acknowledged from the beginning that much of the work would be done at regional rather than national level. Literature has not, however, been accorded the status of other cultural elements.

> Although a Literature Department was established in 1965 *'it was always the poor relation'.*
> (Interview with Alastair Niven previously Director of the Literature Department, Arts Council, England)

And when, in 1984, the *Glory of the garden* (mainly concerned with further devolution to the regions) was published, savings were required to provide funding for the regions and the decision was made to remove the post of Literature Director altogether and scale down the budget by 50%:

> *'English literature ... is sustained by a large and profitable commercial publishing industry. It is the basic ingredient of the schools curriculum. It is available to the public through the public library system ... (the Council) has therefore concluded that its spending on literature should be reduced.*[32]

From 1984-88 there was no central Literature Department and it was up to the regions to continue literature development as they saw fit, from within their own budgets. However, continuous pressure from the regions eventually caused this situation to be reversed. The post of Director was reinstated with a small department and over the past nine years literature has gradually taken on an increasingly high profile with the annual budget increased to some £3 million.

In Wales there is an Arts Council with three regional boards, but neither Scotland nor Ireland have a regional structure. Both Northern Ireland and Wales, whilst supporting workshops, festivals and other activities where writers and readers can meet, lay their stress on support for writers and publishing. Scotland is more active in relation to readers. In 1989 the Scottish Arts Council convened a working party to consider ways and means of extending the readership of literature: *'the writer's creation lies dormant on the printed page, the reader breathes it back to life'*[33] and the Scottish Arts Council supports the major Scottish reading promotion scheme Now Read On.

In Northern Ireland a Verbal Arts Centre has been jointly funded by the North West Education Library Board and the Department of Education since 1992. Its mission: *'to increase awareness of literary heritage, awaken appreciation of verbal heritage and provide opportunity for contemporary verbal arts practice'*. Recently, a proposal was made to extend this to give a province-wide remit with combined funding from the five Education and Library Boards, the Arts Council of Northern Ireland and other bodies. The proposal appears to be going ahead with funding for a co-ordinator agreed.[34]

Over the years, relationships between the Arts Council of England (ACE) and the Regions have been complex. There has been confusion about roles and funding responsibilities. In 1989 Richard Wilding was given the task of conducting a review to investigate, amongst other things: *'the lack of coherence in the formulation and delivery of policy and unwieldy procedures'*. His proposals led to the new autonomous Regional Arts Boards with the recommendation that these should *'delegate much more of their work to local authorities and local associations and make their chief priorities the taking of funding decisions and giving sound advice'*.[35] Their relationship with the ACE was to be federal; the regions would receive their funding on the basis of agreed operational plans which are required to take account of Arts Council priorities but further devolution is gradually placing the funding decisions at regional level, leaving the central role as one of policy-making and strategic development.

This lack of central direction has, however, been criticised :

> *ACE should maintain a national strategic policy role.*
> (Rachel Van Riel   - personal interview)

> *In their support of literature the regional boards are variable. There is a joint literature development officer group but not all regions are represented.*
> (Personal interview Regional Literature Development Officer)

3.3.1 Partnerships with other bodies

Partnerships between the Library Association and ACE have also at times been difficult. Alex Wilson spoke of this:

> *'Despite evidence showing a growing number of libraries were active in that field, the Library Association establishment has long been opposed or at least showed indifference to library /arts involvement'.*[36]

48

In 1985, two library authorities which were particularly active, Sheffield and Birmingham, took the initiative to explore this issue by organizing a conference on partnerships between libraries and the arts. The aim was to discover whether discussions about the potential for an arts/library partnership were being carried through, and a number of resolutions emerged, concerning better working relationships with the regions and the necessity of local authorities having arts policies.[37]

However, despite the number of library authorities which by now were part of leisure departments or involved with a more corporate local authority policy for the development of the arts, Heeks found in her research on these evolving partnerships, that from libraries *'we cannot assume a general enthusiasm for arts partnerships'*. Furthermore, *'answers to specific questions show that a majority of librarians feel no specific commitment to literature'*.[38]

To some extent this is an ongoing saga. The Library Association Public Libraries Committee recently set up a Libraries and Arts working party to consider 'The role of libraries in cultural development.' Their report identifies public libraries as *'essential cultural development agencies within their local community,'* clarifies the 'legitimate role' for libraries in gaining credibility to play their part in social and economic regeneration and claiming a share of competitive funding. For this, evidence is needed on the impact of libraries and a survey of library initiatives in cultural development is proposed, *'to map out the current provision and identify good practice which will then be actively promoted as a basis for general practie.'*[39]

To provide further data in this important area, we asked for comment on the relationships between the Library Association and ACE in the key interviews and how far it was perceived that shared objectives existed:

> *'There are common areas of interest, with the Arts Council conserving the art form and ensuring interest and support from the public - to get people reading. Libraries must surely also want to do this. But it's understandable that literature promotion is only one part of what libraries do and when the chips are down and cuts have to be made it's basically books on shelves that matter.'*
>
> (Alastair Niven, personal interview)

> *'The problem is the LA is a professional body for members. The Arts Council is a publicly funded body with a remit to lead. The library world needs an equivalent to the Arts Council.'*
>
> (Rachel Van Riel, personal interview)

> *'The Arts Council is hugely supportive of public libraries and has worked hard with the library fund. The panel is constantly trying to find ways of making literature accessible.'*
>
> (County Librarian and ACE Literature Panel member, personal interview)

Both the previous Literature Director of ACE, Alastair Niven, and the Chief Executive of the Library Association feel that the partnership on the literature side has never been stronger. Alastair Niven concedes that at one time links between the two organizations were weak and there had been no tradition of working with libraries in his department. Libraries are a statutory service and there were no means by which the Arts Council could fund them directly: the literature department had a very small budget in relation to libraries which meant that any support had to be strategic. It was, however, increasingly recognized that libraries are an outlet:

> *'and they could have a role if it could be identified The impetus came from libraries needing help in promotion and although ACE is not a campaigning body, there are ways of association and support, both strategic and politic. There is now regular communication and in general the Arts Council would welcome ideas for collaborative action.'*

We found that partnerships at regional level were certainly improving. In the questionnaire we asked whether authorities had received funding from any of the Arts Councils for literature promotion: 48% replied in the affirmative whilst 33% said that they were involved with their region in joint initiatives. In several of the regions there are liaison meetings and joint training sessions have become increasingly common. One region has a policy and strategy document that all library authorities and the Regional Arts Board are signed up to and work is being effectively developed across the region as well as with individual authorities. This region organized an international conference on 'Words across Europe'.[40] The West Midlands regional library system is another example - where joint training has been developed[41] and Eastern Arts has recently conducted a training audit for the fifty key staff in the region most likely to be involved in literature promotion. Another region has recently held its first meeting of a newly established reading promotion network with the purpose:

> *'to identify common aims; more people reading, writing and attending events; increased fiction issues, librarians gaining greater confidence in recognising and recommending quality reading.'*
>
> (Regional Literature Officer)

> *'My priority is to work in partnership with library services to raise the standard of reading, to increase confidence in reading and to bring readers together.'*
>
> (Regional Literature Officer)

However, whilst relationships at officer level and in local authorities are improving there still seems to be a lack of awareness at government level of the potential role for libraries in cultural development in general and literature in particular.

> *'It's hinted at in the Commission's 20/20 vision statement but it's absent from the government's agenda. To underline the need for more research into the economic value of libraries and literature would be particularly useful. This is needed not only to convince the government but to give confidence to the profession.'*

(Senior Lecturer, University Department of Library and Information Studies, personal interview)

3.3.2 What is literature?

One of the difficulties in alignment between ACE and public libraries in promoting reading has been in the definition of literature. No one would disagree with the ACE statement that:

> *'The inception of all literature lies in the human imagination and spirit. Our starting point must be ways both written and oral in which these are realised through the creative expression of language.'*[42]

However, ACE is mostly concerned just with modern writing, although in principle it also supports 'heritage' (non-contemporary literature including travel and biography).

> *'The emphasis of ACE is largely about contemporary writing. Generally there is not enough emphasis on the past.'*
>
> (Alastair Niven, personal interview).

Several of the interviewees stated their concerns about the term 'literature', the Arts Council's definition being viewed as elitist by librarians:

> *'Exclusivity has surrounded contemporary literature and can be incestuous. We can be caught up in a false fear of a need to promote the new - a narrow view especially when it's done at the expense of other writing.'*
>
> (Chief Librarian, City Department of Leisure Services, personal interview)

To some extent the former Director for Literature at ACE agreed:

> *'Literature is an elitist word - we're looking for a different one but you can't short - change Shakespeare.'*

Other comments were:

> *'Elitism is a pejorative word and shorthand for all that's seen as bad, but the suggested alternatives can result in patronising attitudes and that's much worse. The assumption that people are unable to read above a certain level because of their backgrounds probably stemmed from a desire to empathise with the community. But it isn't good enough - there's a danger of issues blocking people's opportunities.'*

(Senior Lecturer, University Department of Library and Information Studies, personal interview)

'Snobbery works both ways. The literary establishment is snobbish about popular fiction. The library world has inverted snobbism the other way. The Arts Council has a duty to support the experimental. In the library world there is inverted snobbery. Concentration on reading is the answer, whether a book provides a poor or good reading experience.'

(Rachel Van Riel, personal interview)

'If elitism means quality, then we shouldn't have a problem, but if it means some people feel excluded then it needs to be broken down.'

(County Librarian and ACE panel member, personal interview)

3.3.3 Access

The current strategy of ACE places considerable emphasis on 'access': there has been support for schemes for people with learning difficulties; emphasis has been placed on programmes for ethnic minority communities; and there is a special scheme for work in prisons.The report, *Literature belongs to everyone,* was an attempt to focus on identifying and seeking to remove barriers to literature. The investigation was based on interviews with 62 key people working in institutions that could or ought to be active in opening up literature, including librarians, trade unionists, educationists, arts agencies workers and writers. Again, this pointed to an over- emphasis on new work.

'Access has got to be about the past, not losing the past, 97% of our work in the literature department is to do with new work!'

Over-emphasis on creative writing was also criticised:

'I personally would place the emphasis on reading...creative writing is very important but people will do it if they want to and if they don't read they'll end up as very poor writers. There is no substitute for reading rather a lot.'

Hughes concludes that literature can cover many things: pleasure and escape as well as widening the mind but:

'Access must concentrate on access to the best. However fear of betraying standards of excellence or distorting the true nature of literature lies behind the anxieties. Excellence is a term that needs to be distinguished from elitism. The latter is a social term meaning in practice the exclusion of the minority of people from a social group. Excellence is different.'[43]

3.3.4 Developing literature

The first literature development worker post was set up in 1986, growing out of the writers -in -residence programme. There are now some 40 Literature Development Workers (LDWs) in England, the majority of them library based. Scotland has favoured one- or two -year creative writing posts similar to writers-in-residence and Wales has one post but no national commitment to the concept. LDWs have organized readings and talks about publishing linked with radio and television, acted as information agencies and developed networks, held surgeries for would-be writers and provided training for teachers and for librarians.The National Association for Literature Development (NALD) was formed to provide a network, and information agency and specialist training.

The Ings Report drew attention to one of the major problems for LDWs: short termism. These posts have usually been established in partnership between the Arts Council, the Regional Arts Board and the local authority with 'tapering funding', but with depleted local government funding it has become increasingly difficult to guarantee their continuation. There have also been problems associated with the isolated nature of the posts:[44]

> *'Single unsupported posts are vulnerable; the LDW may soon become exhausted or overstretched.'*

Where posts are renewed :

> *'a change of staff may mean the post has to begin again from scratch.'*

One region has decided to use its funding allocation to work with librarians in training their workers to cover the sort of areas that an outsider might previously have done - an attempt to create an internal culture rather than import a temporary outsider. The Regional Literature Development Officer states:

> *'The literature development movement has always historically put the writer at the centre of development. We don't actually do much for readers except in the sense of audience development for readings by writers. What I am trying to do is use libraries as creative reading development agencies.'*[45]

> *'They (LDWs) are comfortable about writing but don't know much about reader development and need training on this.'*
>
> (Rachel Van Riel, personal interview)

One literature development worker summarized her role as 50% supporting writers, 50% readers, *'though all LDWs work differently.'* Whilst the majority of similar posts are attached in some way to libraries, hers is firmly integrated into the library structure. This she feels is an advantage *'after all the readers and the resources are in libraries'*. The main concern is short termism, and in the view of this LDW, posts should be established for a three-year period to give a reasonable time in which to work whilst not allowing post holders to become stale.

> *'The need for LDWs to work in libraries developing reading is primarily to bring fresh ideas, confidence and a different approach. Coming from a reading rather than a*

library background, I feel that readers are reluctant to talk to librarians about reading because they look busy, you almost feel you must make an appointment!. Whereas in my experience people love to talk about what they are reading and these conversations are casual as I walk through the library.'

(Literature Development Worker- personal interview)

One large authority had a reader-in-residence for some years but this post was cut because of funding problems. Another similar post is currently provided through a combination of City Challenge, Regional Arts and local authority funding. The job description identifies the priorities as :

'...to develop a programme of training which will enable library staff and public to gain skills and confidence in continuing the initiative ... to facilitate a programme of readers' advice surgeries and conversations with members of the public on the subject of fiction.'

(Job description, Reader-in-Residence post)

Joint training sessions are being organized at regional level for literature development workers and librarians :

'Creative reading is where LDWs and librarians can meet.'

(Regional Literature Development Officer)

Another commented;:

'Reader development introduces a whole new area of audience development.'

(Regional Literature Officer)

This joint work appears to be having good effect:

'There is an increasing confidence in library staff to take action rather than leave it to the LDWs.'

(Regional Literature Officer)

3.3.5 Opening the Book

A further example of successful collaboration, at both national and regional levels, came in 1989 when Sheffield organized a major literature festival 'Opening the Book':

'a festival with a difference, using the audience base of libraries. Programmes included meaningful debates rather than author ego outpourings.'

(Rachel. Van Riel, personal interview)

The Arts Council were brought into the thinking at an early stage and supported the festival with a grant of £8000 and also hosted the sponsors' lunch at the Arts Council.

'We had worked very closely with the Literature Director and Literature Officer in the evolution of the Opening the Book concept and achieved mutual interest in the use of public libraries in the development of writing, reading, borrowing and buying of literature.'

(Rachel Van Riel, personal interview)

Three years later, a national conference 'Reading the future: a place for literature in libraries', which has been described as a 'sea change' was held at York. Rachel Van Riel who had been involved with Opening the Book, was asked to devise the programme. Seventy- two senior librarians gathered to hear a strong cast which included A. S. Byatt on 'The irreplaceable importance of reading', a debate on how libraries, publishers and booksellers and library suppliers can work together and two chief librarians speaking on 'How literature fits into public library objectives'. Pat Coleman, then City Librarian of Birmingham, had some strong words to say:

'It's time we reasserted the fundamental facts that libraries are actually about books, about culture, about creativity and that the public library service...is actually one of the major players in the cultural life of the country. Libraries used to have a role but they abdicated it.'

3.3.6 The library fund

It was at this conference that the Library Fund was launched. Perdita Hunt, for the Arts Council, announced that *'the aim of this fund is to promote new practice in libraries in the promotion of literature titles, practice that is lively and forward looking'.*[46] Successful bids included: 'Birmingham Accents', a scheme to promote local writers; 'Building Bridges', targeted promotion in areas of special need in Leeds with training sessions for staff; 'Writers of the Asian Diaspora' in Liverpool; 'Screen and Heard' using film to promote books in Huddersfield; 'A Novel Approach' to increase awareness of contemporary fiction amongst staff and users in Bradford and 'Meeting the Future', a festival of science fiction and fantasy in Cheshire.[47]

Over a three-year period projects have received funding of some £65,000 a year. In 1996 the priorities changed and it was decided to use the Fund to concentrate on identifying literature training needs for librarians and to disseminate information about literature promotion. One result was the first issue of Shelf Talk, a resource pack for librarians. Dependent on interest from libraries a further issue will be produced concentrating on literature promotion in non-library venues, children's work and outreach.

We asked respondents for their views on Shelf Talk; 55% of the authorities have subscribed, but in general they found it difficult to identify *how* they were using it -' it's too early to say'. Some libraries were circulating it to staff and others using it to inspire. One authority stated:

> *'Adult reading promotion is a new concept for many librarians and Shelf Talk will help people to approach it with confidence.'*
>
> (Senior Librarian, County Library Service)

Support from the Arts Council continues for library projects throughout the regions.

We asked the former Literature Director of the Arts Council if there was to be any formal evaluation of the Library Fund initiatives scheme and were told that an evaluative report was under consideration. We also asked why the scheme ended after three years and were told that such schemes are normally short lived.

> *'There were some very good initiatives but they became repetitive. We are now trying to encourage libraries to build literature promotion into their overall library objectives. The LA believes in this and many public libraries are now picking this up. On -offs are useful but the major task is to get literature and reading back on the agenda as mainstream. Creative reading is important - potentially it could include everybody.'*
>
> (Alastair Niven, personal interview)

There was also comment that supported this view, with a call for more objective research to underpin wider initiatives.

> *'There's a need to pull together and analyse all the initiative bids . We need more research on the economic value of reading.'*
>
> (Chief Librarian, City Department of Leisure services, personal interview)

One of the literature panel members when asked about the scheme similarly felt it was difficult to say what had been learned:

> *'One authority's innovation is another's history but initiatives can lead to good practice.'*
>
> (ACE Panel member, personal interview)

There were also criticisms from libraries about unclear criteria and tight deadlines:

> *'There was a lack of clear direction and performance measures. And criteria which were open to different interpretations.'*
>
> (Chief Librarian, personal interview)

However, an alternative view from the Chief Executive of the Library Association was that :

'Challenge schemes are helpful, they require people to work up innovative projects with probably no guarantee of success for the investment of time and energy or continuation when funds dry up .If the criteria are too tight it stifles innovation, if too loose a waste of time but this is how we progress.'

(Chief Executive Library Association, personal interview)

Overall, there was also a new charge of energy and confidence in the library profession and a recognition that promotion can mean something more than a booklist. The part played by the Arts Council as change agent was commented on, albeit with some critical comment:

'ACE has done a tremendous job giving status to libraries. Guidelines and money have helped librarians to see literature promotion as essential, but the Arts Council still don't understand the library world.'

(Rachel Van Riel, personal interview).

Another view, expressed in *Borrowed time*, was the warning that libraries must not be taken over by the Arts Council and turned into literature centres which could *'destroy the very quality that makes public libraries so successful as popular cultural institutions'*.[48]

3.3.7 National lottery funding

Initially, legislation gave public libraries little chance of support from the National Lottery since local authorities' responsibility for libraries is statutory and lottery resources are not intended to replace mainstream funding. However, if a library project were to provide facilities which would not normally be provided or there were a clear partnership with eligible organizations such as Arts or Heritage a library could profit. Some libraries have received such funding, for example for adaptations of library buildings for Arts activities.[49] The new Arts for Everyone rules seem to be rather more flexible and currently a number of authorities are putting together bids - often in partnership with other organizations for promotional schemes.[50] A bid is being prepared under the auspices of the Society of Chief Librarians to include a centralised promotional materials agency, which is further considered in Chapter 5.

3.4 Summary

There are clearly many initiatives for librarians to exploit, with Arts Council support welcomed for the opportunity to experiment and to develop and disseminate good practice. Partnerships at regional level had been particularly fruitful. There was evidence that literature development workers had been important catalysts for change. However, there was concern that the role of the public library should be seen as distinctive and not become confused with that of other organizations.

References

1. Leisure futures. Henley Centre for Forecasting, 1996. In: Book Marketing Ltd. *Book facts 1996: an annual compendium.* London: Book Marketing Ltd 1996, 95.

2. BOOK MARKETING LTD.*Books and the consumer* . London: Book Marketing Ltd. 1996, 41.

3. BOOK MARKETING LTD. *Book facts 1996: an annual compendium.* London: Book Marketing Ltd., 1996, 96 -98.

4. BOOK MARKETING LTD. *Books and the consumer.* London: Book Marketing Ltd., 1994, 33.

5. *Ibid.,* 35

6. Policy Studies Institute survey. *The Times,* March 27th 1997, 6.

7. MANN, M. *The reading habits of adults: a select annotated bibliography.* London: The British Library , 1977. (British National Bibliography Research Fund Report no. 1)

8. MANGUEL, A. *A history of reading.* London: Flamingo, 1996, 149-161.

9. MANN, P. H. *and* J. BURGOYNE. *Books and reading.* London: Deutsch , 1969.

10. MANN P. H. *From author to reader: a social study of books.* London: Routledge and Kegan Paul, 1982, 157.

11. HATT, F. *The reading process: a framework for analysis and description.* London: Bingley, 1976. 13.

12. KARETSKY, S. *Reading research and librarianship: a history and analysis.* New York: Greenwood Press, 1982, xv, 356.

13. GRAY, W. H. *and* R. MONROE. *The reading habits of adults: a preliminary report.* New York: Macmillan, 1929.

14. KARETSKY, *op cit,* 29, 97.

15. *Ibid.,* 313.

16. SIMSOVA, S. Nicholas Rubakin and bibliopsychology. *Libri ,* 16 (2), 1966,118-29 reprinted in S. Simsova and J. S. Kujoth. *Libraries, readers and book selection,* Metuchen, N.J.: Scarecrow Press, 1969.

17. VAN RIEL, R. *and* O. FOWLER. *Opening the book: finding a good read.* Bradford: Bradford Libraries, 1996.

18. KARETSKY, *op. cit.,* 287.

19. SAYERS, W. C. B. What people read. *Library World,* 38 (21) 1936, 232-234.

20. MUNFORD, W. A. The public library in the social survey. *Library Association Record,* 37, 1937, 410 -414.

21. MANN, P. H. *op cit.,* 157.

22. BREWIS, W.L.E., Geriche, E. M. and Geriche, J. A. Reading needs and motives of adult users of fiction ,*Mousain ,* 12 (2), 3-18 .

23. MCCLELLAN, A. W. The reading dimension in effectiveness and service. *Library Review,* 30,1981,78.

24. NELL, V. *Lost in a book; the psychology of reading for pleasure.* New Haven: Yale University Press, 1988, 256.

25. WIEGARD, W. A. Taste cultures and librarians: a position paper, *Drexel Library Quarterly,* 16(3), 1980, 1-11

26. ZAAIMAN, R. B. Light or enlightened reading, *South African Journal of Library and Information Science,* 49(2), 1981, 47.

27. LUCKHAM. B. How constant are the readers? In: P. Kaegbein, B. Luckham and V. Stelmach, eds. *Studies on research in reading and libraries.* Paris: K G Saur, 1991, 239.

28. COMEDIA. *Borrowed time? The future of public libraries in the U K.* Stroud: Comedia, 1993.

29. O'ROURKE, R. Unpopular readers: the case for genre fiction. Stroud: Comedia, 1993, 3-4.

30. SABINE, G. *and* P. SABINE. *Books that make a difference, what people told us.* New York: Library Professional Publications, 1983.

31. HAMSHERE, S. J. Exploration and escape: the needs fulfilled by borrowing books from a public library. M.A. dissertation.Sheffield University, Department of Information Studies, 1990, 4.

32. ARTS COUNCIL OF GREAT BRITAIN. *The glory of the garden: the development of the arts in England: strategy for a decade.* London: The Arts Council of Great Britain, 1984, 29.

33. SCOTTISH ARTS COUNCIL. *Readership report: a document prepared by the Working Party of the Literature Committee of the Scottish Arts Council.* Edinburgh: Scottish Arts Council, 1986.

34. LIBRARY AND INFORMATION SERVICES COUNCIL (NORTHERN IRELAND) AND VERBAL ARTS CENTRE LTD. *Verbal arts development in libraries and schools.* Belfast: LISC (NI), 1996.

35. SPIERS, H. ed. *Libraries and the arts in partnership.* Stamford: Capital Planning Information, 1990, 3.

36. *Ibid.*, 1.

37. COLEMAN, P. M., ed. *Libraries and the arts: an evolving partnership.* London: Library Association, 1987, 45.

38. HEEKS, P. *Public Libraries and the arts:an evolving partnership.* London: Library Association, 1989.

39. LIBRARY ASSOCIATION PUBLIC LIBRARIES COMMITTEE. LIBRARIES AND THE ARTS WORKING PARTY. The role of libraries in cultural development. Unpublished paper. London: Library Association, 1997.

40. SHEPHERD, J. *and* J. TASKER, eds. *Words across Europe partnership. Report and recommendations.* Northampton: Northamptonshire County Council, 1997.

41. WARREN, G. Developing together in literature promotion: an evaluation of collaborative training for public library staff in the West Midlands 1995-6. Unpublished paper, 1996.

42. ARTS COUNCIL OF ENGLAND. *Literature grants 1996/7.* London: Arts Council of England,1996.

43. HUGHES, V. M. *Literature belongs to everyone. A report on widening access to literature.* London:Arts Council of Great Britain.

44. INGS, R. *Report on the literature development worker movement.* London: Arts Council of Great Britain,1992, 6, 24-38.

45. WATSON, D. Empowering literary choice. *Library Association Record*, 98(9), 1996.

46. VAN RIEL, R. *Reading the future: a place for literature in public libraries. A report of the seminar held in York March 1992, organised by the Arts Council of Great Britain in association with the Library Association and the Regional Arts Boards of England.*London: The Library Association,1992, 33, 84.

47. STEWART, I. *Shelf talk :promoting literature in public libraries.* London: The Arts Council of England /The Library Association, 1996.

48. GREENHALGH, L. and K. Worpole with C. Landry. *Libraries in a world of cultural change.*London: UCL.Press, 1995, 83.

49. *Cultural Trends.* Books, libraries and reading 24 (6), 1996,27.

50. Arts Council of England. *Arts 4 everyone.* London: The Arts Council of England, 1997

4. Public library responses

How libraries are responding to the challenges posed by the book trade, with evidence of the borrowing patterns being achieved, is discussed in this chapter. Further consideration of policy on reading promotion also develops the argument in Chapter 2, with reference here to staffing and education and training.

4.1 Libraries and bookshops

It has always been assumed that book buying and book borrowing were in competition but England and Sumsion note that:

> '*Books and the consumer* has consistently shown that such an assumption is difficult to sustain. In almost all respects those who use libraries are more likely to be book buyers than those who do not'.

This is also borne out by recent MORI polls which show remarkably similar figures for visitors to bookshops and libraries.[1]

There is evidence that 80% of adults bought books from shops in 1995 and some 20% bought by post: an increase of 2% from 1989. One-third of the purchases were for children and 37% of buyers buy 16 or more books a year, between them purchasing 76% of all books sold. In 1995, 59% of the adult population bought for themselves - an increase of 11% on 1989 figures - whilst 40% bought for another adult - an increase of 1% - and 43% for a child, an increase of 2%.[2] According to the Policy Studies Institute money spent on books has almost doubled from £948 million in 1985 to £1.7 billion in 1996.[3] The amount spent on marketing rose from £31,000 in 1981 to £888,000 in 1993.[4]

Worpole puts the increase in book buying down to relative cheapness.

> '*Today the average hard back novel costs perhaps 5% of the average weekly wage and a new paperback novel 2%. Second hand bookshops buy, sell or exchange genre fiction for as little as 20p.*'[5]

He draws attention to the paperback revolution and argues that in a relatively affluent society it is necessary to re-examine the role of the 'free' lending library.

That society views books as consumables is undoubtedly another major factor. These days books are available in supermarkets, at garages, at airports. Many people with money to spend prefer to purchase their reading matter and then discard it or pass it on to friends rather than have the responsibility of keeping it safe and returning it on time to the library. This way they can obtain their social reading quickly - the best seller or highly reviewed book - particularly if it is available in paperback. But it is not only affluence and the convenience of the bookshop which is swaying people in that direction. In *Borrowed time*, the authors cite evidence to suggest that some people prefer bookshops because of the ambiance.[6]

In the questionnaire we asked about statements relating to the attractiveness of book shops *vis a vis* libraries in order to probe how far librarians recognized this issue:

`The public library will be unable to compete with the commercial bookshops activities because:'

TABLE 9: *Libraries and perceived competition from bookshops*

Statement	strongly agree %	neither strongly agree nor disagree %	strongly disagree %
The ambiance of bookshops is preferable	21	26	51
The public feel they can ask for help in selection in bookshops	6	16	75
The trade know what is of current interest	20	31	48
Bookshops attract ... staff recruited on the basis of their enthusiasm for books and ideas	20	27	51

Two authorities felt unable to comment since they disagreed with the overall statement. We also asked for comment on these statements in our interviews, with concern expressed at the way libraries had fallen behind in their effective use of 'atmospherics' to enhance library use:

> *Libraries vary hugely in size and feel; more could be done without much money with guiding and signing.*
> (Chief Executive, Library Association, personal interview)

> *Bookshops' arrangements are often nicely muddled giving a sense of discovery.*
> (Chief Librarian, Department of Leisure Services, City authority, personal interview)

> *Public libraries are starved of capital, they don't look modern and attractive. Marketing is 'looks' in book shops.*
> (Manager, Waterstones bookshop, personal interview)

Many branch libraries for economic reasons have not been refurbished and have a '60s image - there are techniques that bookshops use which are finding their way into libraries.

(Head of University Library and Information Studies Department, personal interview)

Some felt, though, that it would be wrong for libraries to adopt the 'branding' of a successful book chain:

Appropriateness to individual communities is important. One Smiths or Waterstones is very much like another.

(Chief Executive, Library Association, personal interview)

We also asked for comment on the suggestion that the public find it easier to ask for help in selection because they are paying for it and that bookshops *'attract ... staff recruited on the basis of their enthusiasm for books.'*[7]

People do feel they can ask for help if they are paying.

(Chief Librarian, Leisure Services Department, personal interview)

Paying for help is probably a red herring, it's more a question of public confidence and staff knowledge . How many library staff could now function as readers' advisors?

(Senior Lecturer, University Information and Library Studies Department, personal interview)

They do have staff with enthusiasm; trained and paid to promote. We could learn how to sell books from the trade.

(County Librarian, personal interview)

We could learn a lot from their enthusiasm but librarians have a more in-depth knowledge than they realise.

(Chief Librarian Leisure Services Department, personal interview)

Worpole argued that bookshops have often been a place for stimulating discussion, advertising meetings, organizing readings and book launches and taking a much more active role than simply selling books.[8]

Meanwhile, the multiples such as Waterstones are increasingly entering into programmes of book signings, and author talks and most recently reading groups. The manager of a branch of Waterstones clarified that their promotional strategies are largely the result of customer feedback, that their target audience are heavy bookbuyers and that they would not normally stock material which is outside this profile. A core stock list was generated from computerized information on sales, to help in deciding stock levels. In recruiting staff, management concentrates on finding people who are readers and can give a good account of their reading. They are expected to continue and develop their interest and to have a general awareness of current affairs and cultural trends. Their centralized marketing department involves retail staff in developing promotions and whilst local managers have a fair degree of autonomy they are expected to use these and *'not to do their own thing on the lines of Blue Peter!'* Training in display is viewed as very important and is provided by the central marketing department. In the view of this manager *'Presentation IS marketing'*. (Interview with the manager Waterstones Bookshop Leicester.)

4.2 The Net Book Agreement

While large chains can provide such centralized support and rely heavily on volume for profit, smaller bookshops were felt to be more dependent on the protection afforded by the Net Book Agreement (NBA). In September, 1995, when the NBA collapsed, there was grave speculation. Those who supported the NBA were concerned lest its abolition would lead to a reduction in titles published and also harm the small bookseller who would not have the turnover to give discount. Those who favoured abolition based their arguments on the prospect of increased sales from more outlets and to a wider public. So far it would appear that neither effect has happened. Bookwatch, a monitoring organization, reported an increase of 25% in sales in the first two months after the ending of the agreement and then a return to normal or only slightly below normal.

> *The net effect is zero. The market is stable and hasn't changed in 15 years. Prices rise and fall but it barely affects sales. People buy the books they can read and not much more or less.*[9]

However, there are implications which may not at first be apparent. According to one library supplier profit margins are now so tight that the 'benefit in kind' that has long been part of the relationship between public libraries and library suppliers; publicity materials, author visits, displays and exhibitions and complex servicing requirements will no longer be possible if librarians insist on maximum discount - as we noted in Chapter 2.

4.3 Public library borrowing

The *Books and the consumer* survey shows that 28% of adults borrowed a book at least every 3-4 weeks, while 25% borrowed less frequently. Ten per cent of weekly borrowers take 43% of the books borrowed and the majority of library users are fiction readers. Non -fiction is borrowed more by men and more frequently by people under 25. There are heavy library users with 16% of all borrowers accounting for 50% of all issues and 37% of borrowers for 85%. There is therefore a small but significant section of the community which uses public libraries to a considerable extent.[10] The Public Lending Right (PLR) analysis of types of books borrowed in 1988/9 and 1994/5 is shown below. It again describes a fall in light romance reading, with children's fiction showing a rise in issues:[11]

TABLE 10: *Public library book issues*

	1988/9	1994/5
ADULT FICTION		
General Fiction	17.8	20.8
Historical	3.5	3.7
Mystery and detection	12.8	13.4
Horror	0.7	0.6
Science Fiction	0.8	0.9
War	1.8	1.3
Humour	0.7	0.3
Light romance	14.1	11.9
Westerns	1.2	0.8
Short stories	0.5	0.3
NON FICTION		
Science and technology	1.3	0.9
History	3	2.7
Travel and foreign countries	2.9	2.5
Social Sciences	2.5	2.2
Religion	0.9	0.8
Nature and Country life	1.5	1.2
Domestic and leisure	4.7	4.0
Health	1.7	1.7
The Arts	1.2	0.9
Biography	2.6	2.7
Humour	0.7	0.3
Literature	0.9	0.7
All	24.4	20.6
Children's books	21.7	25.4
All		

The PLR statistics also reveal that there are no literary top names in the top 100 books issued by public libraries. Mann estimated from Euromonitor surveys that probably only 1.6% of men and 4% of women read serious fiction, which he defined for research purposes as *'written by a British author - serious in intent author who wants to be judged by critical literary standards rather than market success'*.

In his report to the Arts Council, he showed that on a sample of 100 readers of serious modern fiction the readers were mainly younger women, well educated and of social classes A and B. One-third of these novels were chosen because they 'looked interesting' but only 40% were enjoyed, whereas when author and title were known to the reader there was a 92% satisfaction rate. Where the author only was known this was 67%.[12]

While the popularizing of literary awards has developed in the years since this report was published (1980), there are still undoubtedly lessons to be learned by librarians in simply communicating to their readership about new authors and new fiction. Library users feel more comfortable with authors they know; encouraging exploration in reading is therefore an important role for libraries.

4.4 Library policies on reading

We followed up this concern in our analysis of library policy statements. In the survey, as we stated in Chapter 2, 31% of the respondents had policy statements which included reference to their role in reading promotion. Many of the book selection policy documents also included statements which acknowledged a responsibility for satisfying reading needs rather than merely responding to demand:

> *To provide enjoyment; to contribute towards the intellectual, emotional, psychological and social development of the individual; to enable the acquisition and development of critical awareness of knowledge, values and attitudes; to reflect individual, local, national and global values and experiences; to assist in the preservation of cultural heritage; to provide a vicarious experience of life in terms of time, place and culture; to encourage an appreciation of human achievement and aspirations; to assist the creative and scientific enquiry process; to embrace the concept of intellectual freedom; to understand their own and other people's situations.*
>
> (Book selection policy document, County library service)

> *... to stimulate imagination; to foster creativity; to improve literacy and develop the reading habit.*
>
> (Book selection policy document, London Borough)

From this, we concluded that more work was needed by library managers to define their policy in relation to book selection and promotion regimes, given that more than two-thirds of public library authorities were unable to provide documentary evidence of their policy on book promotion. There was felt to be a need to return to the basics of professionalism with specific regard to book promotion and selection policies: the bedrock of effective public library provision and the means of developing the significant role of reading encouragement.

4.4.1 Reading: the role of librarians

Getting back to this position of core provision means that public librarians will need fundamentally to reassess their roles, roles which have increasingly been shaped by the information technology revolution. Internet connections have taken the high ground of professional concern in recent years. Snape, for example, states that though most business transacted in libraries is books borrowed primarily for leisure reading this is not as highly valued by librarians as other aspects of their service:

'For the last 15 years the library profession has redefined its self image in close alignment with information and particularly with information technology ... the public libraries' leisure function ... has not featured largely in the professional press ... research in librarianship is heavily biased towards information management'.[13]

There is also the problem that fiction provision has been regarded as a waste of public funds. Atkinson emphasised that for over 130 years there had been a controversy regarding the provision of fiction which was regarded as frivolous, a waste of money, but quotes E. A. Baker who wrote in 1899

Prose fiction now constitutes a permanent part of the library. It is more used than any other, and the library that did away with it would deprive itself of the readiest means of interest and popularity.[14]

Atkinson also noted that, as far back as 1938, H. S. A. Smith addressed a conference of British librarians, calling for a *'scientific delineation of the effects of books'* but he maintained that this was outside the competence of librarians and that research should be carried out by sociologists and psychologists.[15]

Luckham felt that *'If changes in what people read is possible or desirable the first condition must be a detailed account of what they read'* - although once again the role of librarians in amassing these data was not made clear.[16] Comedia, too, criticize the profession which has

chosen to exclude itself from many of the most important developments in post-war literacy, concerns which have moved away from the writer to the creative role of the reader.

They question why librarians are marginal to Arts Council thinking on cultural policies and absent from the panels of literary prizes or poetry competitions and warn that the idea of literature centres is an indication of lack of confidence in what used to be acknowledged as fundamental to public libraries. They also criticize librarians about their indecisiveness concerning genre fiction and go on to say that without a better understanding of what readers are deriving from their reading patterns *'formulating policies about fiction stock is impossible'.*[17]

Much of this criticism might seem unfair to librarians, who after all are not sociologists, but it does point up the need for librarians to exploit the available research data more thoroughly and to take more account of findings when setting policy. It also highlights the importance of posts which are dedicated to readers' needs, with professionals in place who can support readers and feed back their concerns to management.

4.4.2 Advising readers

In the survey we found, though, that only 10% of authorities had posts designated as readers' advisor, which accorded with the apparent demand as noted by Jennings and Sear who found that a mere 8% of users asked the help of the librarian in selecting books.[18] This is also reflected in Spiller's study.[19]

Readers' advisors appeared to have all but vanished. In tracing the history of this role, Kelly notes the emphasis that started to be placed on reference work, post war.[20] An important development was the job of 'readers' advisor' distinguished at this time as something separate and specific. Foskett argued that merging reference and lending functions was a mistake since it was via the lending library that most readers made their first acquaintance with the library.[21] Prytherch, however, felt that:

> all contact between staff and users has the potential to develop into enquiry work ... in this informal way the majority of the users will prefer to approach the staff, a 'formal' arrangement to speak to a reader' advisor will deter more than encourage.[22]

This was borne out by Blake, in a study of Wincanton library, who revealed that 19% of the enquiries concerned author/title, and 30% 'material': the remainder were directional or information enquires. The low number of author /title enquiries is noted, the explanation being that users were content to browse through the shelves rather than ask for a specific book. Thirteen per cent of queries concerned arts/humanities and social sciences and these were often 'literary based concerning sections of book stock'. Out of 106 enquiries, staff knowledge was used in 17 cases 'several users asked what certain books were like. In some of these cases staff could give their opinion'.[23]

Karetsky states that the readers' advisory movement in the USA started in the 1920s, the duties 'to select reading materials for individuals and groups that had a serious desire for education'. The movement grew in the 1930s but came under wide attack by librarians because of the rationale, the methods of working and the expense, and increasingly the advisory function became diffused throughout the library. The main proponents of the readers' advisor were concerned with the reading research movement; they saw this as a means of practising action research: 'an effective readers' advisory service necessitated knowledge of the adult's relationship to books and reading, and

consequently the advisors were the experts among practising librarians'
but readers' advisors' had a negative view of scientific methods, seeing
this as *'distasteful and limited in productivity ... The amount of data
advisors collected from their patrons varied. Many obtained much
information but others were loathe to pry'.*[24]

It was emphasised that only through years of experience could
librarians learn how readers reacted to books.

Ross notes that the old style readers' advisor, concerned with
promoting reading with a purpose, *'interviewing clients, drawing up an
individualised annotated reading list designed to provide a variety of
viewpoints whilst leading the reader in orderly consecutive steps from an
introduction to more complex treatments'*, lost support for a number of
reasons including: the increased attention paid to information storage and
retrieval and a reaction against improving people's taste in reading,
which was seen as elitism. Recent thinking, however, has redefined the
role in the USA as one which pays attention to both books and reader.
More than one hundred open-ended qualitative interviews were used to
show how users find books and how books help people and Ross
concluded that people need guidance and that librarians can facilitate
selection by paying closer attention to how people choose. The evidence
shows that *'readers know what kind of reading experience they want and
will simply ignore any advice that does not take their preferences into
account'*, and that a book which suits a reader in a particular situation is
a good book.[25]

Attention is drawn to a growing body of research which confirms that
readers improve their reading *by* reading, as Meek points out: *'readers
need to know many books: each one becomes more significant as it joins
the others that have been read before'.*[26] However, Ross found that *'the
public does not think of librarians as experts who can recommend good
books for leisure reading'* citing a survey in which 'recommended by a
librarian' came nineteenth out of thirty-eight possible factors influencing
selection. Readers use book shops to pre-select from a smaller number of
books which they then attempt to borrow from libraries. Librarians
should therefore be more active in bridging the gap between the reader's
needs and the library, by: advertising willingness to help, developing
readers' advisory skills, facilitating browsing, encouraging readers to
share enthusiasms and encouraging staff to read. Adopting some of the
mechanisms that book shops use to appeal to impulse buyers are
suggested as ways in which librarians might be more proactive in the
selection process.[27]

In the period between 1950 and 1980 many library administrators in the USA phased out readers' advisory services on grounds of cost effectiveness. *'Library administrators felt they could save money by having their reference librarian answer reference and readers advisory questions',*[28] a situation found too in the UK, when the need for staffing cutbacks in recent years has meant the growth of professional generalism and a move away from specialist posts.

It is noted in the USA that currently there is a resurgence of the readers' advisor, reflecting librarians' concerns about users being overwhelmed by choice. Because of shortage of funds the new readers' advisor is using techniques which help more than one reader at a time, e.g., book talks, lists, displays, etc., as a substitute for individual assistance. Although in our survey only 10% of authorities had named posts, there was some evidence that this masked a more positive picture. One authority stated that all staff working on the desk were deemed to be readers' advisors.

However, we recorded some strong views on advice to readers:

'Advice means offering suggestions not impelling people to take specific action.
(Alistair Niven - personal interview)

There is a belief that the reader doesn't need help, therefore it's patronising to offer it. Librarians are more at home in a pedagogic rather than a recreational context.
(Rachel Van Riel - personal interview)

4.5 Training and education

As staff roles were such a crucial factor in determining the effectiveness of promotion and support for readers we were interested in the availability and nature of training in library authorities. Given the lack of funding at present, it was encouraging that 62% of library authorities offered some level of training, although it was felt this needed to be improved for such a key function.

TABLE 11: *Training in reading promotion*

	%
Overall	62
In house	20
Externally	26
Both	80

Van Riel argues that until literature promotion is written into librarians' job descriptions too much will depend on individual enthusiasm and initiative.The training courses provided by 'Opening the book' are said to give 'confidence rather than knowledge'.[29] Some fifty authorities have used this independent training organization, and comments are almost always favourable; *'after attending a course, staff felt they could conquer the world'* (Chief Librarian,Leisure Services Department - personal interview) and *'Promoting fiction ... is in our business plan for the year, there is no existing expertise or tradition in our organization so updating knowledge and enhancing skills was the main reason for attending'.* (Team Leader, County Authority - questionnaire response)

Sometimes, though, lack of structure means that initial enthusiasm is not channelled into action:

> *One member of staff attended the `training the trainers' course with a view to carrying out some reading promotion. Because of changes in job responsibilities this hasn't happened.*
>
> (District Librarian - questionnaire response)

Van Riel feels that courses are more valuable when there is follow up, one workshop is not enough. It is essential that the concepts and approach are understood *'rather than too much reliance on charisma and confidence building or encouragement'.* (Rachel Van Riel - personal interview)

The key to success in these courses seems to be the exploration of attitudes to reading. A book may be difficult or boring, upsetting, slow to get into. The risks in recommending books are also identified, staff might be found to be lacking in knowledge, their personal tastes might be exposed, recommendations could be seen as endorsement of one book over another.Van Riel, however, cautions that any feeling of 'responsibility' is unnecessary. Readers can 'try out' any number of books before they find the book they are seeking: *'borrowers need reassurance that there's no stigma or sense of failure in not finishing a book'.*[30]

Training in literature promotion is currently also a priority for the Arts Council of England's Library Fund.

The West Midlands Regional Library system has co-ordinated training in literature promotion on behalf of the eleven authorities in the region. Eight sessions were run, each organized by a different authority: How to run an arts/literature event, Write on ... promoting black literature in libraries, Asian literature promotion, Story telling for all ages, Poetry on the Internet; Taking Risks - dilemmas in stock selection, Reading in its own right and Working with parents to help children enjoy books. The evaluation states that objectives were achieved in that all library authorities participated, regional writers and trainers were used, cultural diversity was acknowledged and the whole was considered to be a more effective use of Arts Council funding than one-off public events.[31] Similar training has been provided in other regions, including the North West Arts Board and Yorkshire and Humberside Arts Boards. One programme consisted of seven sessions on topics like creative reading: raising the status of reading, increasing people's confidence in reading, bringing isolated readers together and literature development and live literature promotion; literature development and libraries, models of good practice, links with publishers and promotions and managing the event.

In order to widen the professional base of literature promotion the Literature Department of the Arts Council of England commissioned research in 1995 to develop and implement a proposal for an accredited literature module for librarianship courses. The report of this work acknowledges the role played by libraries in the promotion of books and reading and the Arts Council support in assisting public libraries to promote contemporary literature. It does however state that *'Without long term development of literature expertise amongst library staff literature development will remain sporadic and dependent upon individual skills and enthusiasm'*. Noting the short courses which have been provided, it argues for training to be formalised and provided at an earlier stage in professional development and reiterates the recommendations stemming from the' Reading the future' conference which identified the need to counter the present tendency to make information more important than literature and argued for a re-emphasis on developing in degree courses a love of reading and the ability to communicate this by *'educating as well as responding to readers' reading needs and preferences'*. The intention was to develop an optional module focusing on the promotion of contemporary imaginative literature. The report is critical of librarians' existing knowledge of literature and states that the role of the librarian in advising readers is an important one. In order to accomplish this they should be able to draw on a body of literary knowledge and experience.

The conclusion is that, at present, information technology monopolises the curriculum, however, *'there remains within a number of library schools a strong commitment to retaining public libraries on the curriculum and to maintaining and developing literature focused units of study'*. In analyzing existing courses the conclusion is reached that:

> *'none really embrace the concept of literature promotion in libraries as a coherent package. Such a package would cover the landscape of contemporary literature, of books and reading guides, from critical evaluation of text to proactive promotion, establishing literary merit and diversity as opposed to user expectations as the criteria'*.

The module proposed focuses on trends and developments in British writing in the last five years, planning a literature strategy in libraries, libraries and the arts infrastructure, strategies to promote the book and marketing and audience development .

The recommendations suggested piloting the module in two library schools, the development of a consortia or network of library schools and other interested agencies and the development of generic teaching resources.[32] The module has been trial run by the University of Central England School of Information Studies and Sheffield University Department of Information Studies. The Arts Council comments:

> On the basis of the trial, an unexpectedly high take up resulted. Librarians can't be expected to have a background in literature but they must be in a position to advise and it should be central to their training, technology is important but it shouldn't be at the expense of reading.
>
> (Alistair Niven, personal interview)

The Library Association welcome, the initiative, but:

> what inhibits development is that all schools show evidence that few students want to work in public libraries, the reasons being the depressed state of local government and the dearth of jobs.
>
> (Chief Executive, Library Association - personal interview)

However it is felt that the tendency for departments to enable students to select pathways from a set of modules rather than a set course would make this a more viable option. Where schools have a special interest in public libraries this would be more feasible and there is scope for more sophisticated courses to link between initial training and work-specific training. Sheffield Department of Information Studies is pleased with the module both in terms of take- up and commitment. Some comments from students include: *'wonderful - hope you run it again and again'* and *'excellent initiative - good idea to have a prom - lit library'*... *'the most worthwhile course I've taken for a long time'*. In this case the Arts Council funding has made it possible to run the module, however it is felt that there will not be available resources within the university to continue once the external funding has been withdrawn.

The University of Central England emphasised the usefulness of the recognition by the Arts Council and the additional funding which has paid for external speakers and provided an extensive range of popular contemporary fiction. At this university an optional module in popular fiction was already offered for undergraduate and masters courses.[33] These have run for some time and therefore the trial module was, with agreement, incorporated into the course. The only element which was added to the existing syllabus was literary criticism, whilst promotion was extended. Whilst it is emphasised that:

> *it is important that students read the books for themselves rather than a large number of critical textbooks it will be useful to give students an insight into traditional and contemporary literary criticism. An examination of fiction reviewing will also be undertaken and in the next academic year it is hoped to incorporate reading non fiction for pleasure, e.g., biography, travel writing etc.*
> (Senior Lecturer Department of Library and Information Studies, personal interview)

Both universities were asked about the potential for developing the module to the needs of continuing education. Whilst it was recognised that there was potential for distance learning, perhaps with the use of the Internet, there was some uncertainty about the willingness of authorities or students to pay. The Library Association on the other hand felt that

> *distance learning is growing and this could be a possibility. There is scope for more sophisticated courses to link between initial training and work specific interest. This would give a good bridge and could be taught on site - but financing could be a problem .*
> (Chief Executive, Library Association - personal interview)

Comments on research in this subject area were also made.

> *Public libraries have been poorly served by research and this has not helped reading promotion. There is potential for more research with colloborative working with public libraries, library schools and bodies like the Arts Council.*
> (Head of Department Information and Library Studies - personal interview.)

The future of training is a difficult matter to resolve, though, given the lack of resourcing for training and the shift towards a more IT-based curriculum in initial education:

> *It may be a matter for open learning...but librarians <u>must</u> be passionate about books and their power to change lives.*
> (Chief Librarian, City Leisure Services Department - personal interview)

Line's proposal for a common course for booksellers and librarians is one possibility. He felt that there were many elements in common, considerable support in the commercial sector and a sizeable market for an undergraduate course and quite possibly a postgraduate one.[34] National Vocational Qualifications have also been suggested as a way forward but these appear to have developed along the lines of basic customer care, business and administrative practices and management. Currently, it would appear that there is nothing which would contain the book knowledge and knowledge of readers and reading promotion which are central to this topic. This was substantiated by the bookseller and library suppliers interviewed as well as by library managers.

The Open College of the Arts is about to pilot a module on reading as part of its arts for leisure courses and there have been suggestions of looking into the possibity of using of the BBCs Learning Zone space for training. Both of these initiatives could offer possible ways forward.

4.6 Summary

While the book trade does pose challenges to the public library's role in an increasingly consumer-oriented society, public libraries continue to meet reading needs. Leisure reading remains a core part of library use, despite an increased emphasis on information provision and the use of technology in recent years. Staffing of libraries needs to reflect this, with more resourcing for in-service training. Schools of Library and Information Studies also need to ensure that students entering public library work have an insight into reading for leisure and informal education and in-depth knowledge of fiction and the professional tasks of book selection and promotion, together with other stock management issues.

References

1. ENGLAND, L. *and* J. SUMSION. *Perspectives of public library use: a compendium of survey information.* London: Book Marketing Ltd, Loughborough: Loughborough University, Library and Information Statistics Unit, 1995, 16.
2. BOOK MARKETING LTD. *Book facts.* London: Book Marketing Ltd, 1996, 41-42.
3. *Cultural Trends,* 24, 25 March, 1997.
4. BOOK MARKETING LTD, *op cit*, 20.
5. WORPOLE, K. *The public library and the bookshop.* Working paper 3. Stroud: Comedia, 1993, 3.
6. COMEDIA. *Borrowed time? The future of public libraries in the United Kingdom.* Stroud: Comedia, 1993, 74, 44.
7. WORPOLE, *op c*it, 7.
8. *Ibid.*
9. *Cultural Trends, op cit* , 20.
10. BOOK MARKETING LTD, *op cit*, 86.
11. ENGLAND, L. *and* R. SUMSION, *op cit.*
12. MANN, P. H. *The literary novel and its public. Report to the Arts Council LiteraturePanel.* Sheffield: University of Sheffield, 1980, 83.
13. SNAPE. R. Home reading, *In:* Kinnell, M. *and* Sturges, P., eds. *Continuity and innovation in the public library : the development of a social institution.* London: Library Association Publishing, 1996, 67.
14. ATKINSON, F. *Fiction librarianship.* London: Bingley, 1981.
15. SMITH, H. S. A. *In:* Atkinson, F. *Fiction librarianship.* London: Bingley, 1981, 12.
16. LUCKHAM, B. How constant are the readers? *In:* Kaegbein, P., B. Luckham *and* V. Stelmach, eds. *Studies on research in reading and libraries.* Paris: K. G. Saur, 1991, 17.
17. COMEDIA, *op cit,* 48.
18. JENNINGS, B. *and* L. SEAR. How readers select fiction: a survey in Kent. *Public Libraries Journal,* 4, 1986, 43-7.

19. SPILLER, D. The provision of fiction in public libraries. *Journal of Librarianship*, 12 (4), 1980, 226-38.
20. KELLY, T. *History of public libraries in Great Britain 1845-1965.* London: Library Association, 1973.
21. FOSKETT. D. J. *Assistance to readers in lending libraries.* London: Library Association, 1952, 38.
22. PRYTHERCH, R. *The basics of readers' advisory work.* London: Bingley, 1988, 99.
23. BLAKE, N. *Enquiry statistics: an analysis of enquiries asked at selected public and special libraries in the U K.* Loughborough: Loughborough University Library and Information Statistics Unit, 1995, 33.
24. KARETSKY, S. *Reading research and librarianship: a history and analysis.* New York: Greenwood Press, 1982.
25. ROSS, C. S. Readers' advisory service: new directions. *R. Q.*, 30 (4) Summer, 1991, 503-518.
26. MEEK, M. *Learning to read.* London: Bodley Head 1982.
27. ROSS, *op cit*, 509.
28. SPILLER, *op cit*
29. VAN RIEL, R. Why promote. In: Stewart, I. *Shelf talk: promoting literature in public libraries.* London: The Arts Council of England/ The Library Association, 1996, 1.03.
30. *Ibid.*
31. WARREN, G. *Developing together in literature promotion. An evaluation of collaborative training for public library staff in the west Midlands, 1995-6.* Birmingham: West Midlands Regional Library System, 1996.
32. HICKS. D. *Research project to develop and implement a proposal for an accredited literature module for librarianship courses.* London: Arts Council of England, 1995.
33. DENHAM. D. Back to basics; training and education opportunities for the exploitation of fiction in public libraries. *Public Libraries Journal*, 11 (3), 1996, 77-80.
34. LINE, M. B. *Education and training for the book and information world.* London: British Library, 1990. (British National Bibliography Research Fund Report 45)

5. Marketing and promoting reading

A wider range of marketing techniques, together with enhancement of the more traditional promotional tools such as displays and book lists, have developed in libraries over the past fifteen years. In this chapter we discuss our findings against this background of an increased acceptance that libraries have to become more customer-focused, with the need for more effective take-up of marketing. The overall concept of marketing embraces the range of activities from planning through to service design and delivery. As just one of the marketing 'mix' tools, promotion is frequently taken to be synonymous with all marketing activity. Here, we focus mainly on promotion, while examining its functions in this wider context.

5.1 The role of marketing and reading promotion

... the characteristic of neutrality may be hampering the library and preventing innovation within the service. The ideal of neutrality goes together with that of universal provision and both ideals can be restraints to a more active and targeted promotion of library services.[1]

Phelan states that it was not until the 1980s that reading promotion became identifiable in public libraries. It is suggested that this was in tune with most local authority services which had little sense of marketing and a 'lacklustre approach' to publicity and promotion. Leaving aside children's libraries where it has always been a core activity, Phelan puts the development down to a new emphasis on marketing which came into vogue during that period - largely driven by the consequences of government legislation and the influence of arts marketing. Specific mention is made of the Southern Arts promotion which led to 'Well Worth Reading'.[2]

The influence of the book trade can also be noted, particularly in promotion and presentation. Baverstock argues that marketing books is not conceivably different from any other type of for -profit marketing. Books are product lines, and to be successful the trade has to engage in market research, segment the market and devise an overall marketing strategy and a marketing plan.[3] In *How to market books*, she also gives clear guidance on promotion.[4] The development of market research in the book trade is evident from the work of Bookmarketing Ltd which took over from the Publishers Association in 1990 and, as we have discussed earlier, now produces reports and statistics continuously via *Books and the consumer*.[5] The increase in the amount spent on advertising in the book trade is phenomenal: advertising expenditure for book-shops has risen in five years by 234.6% from £650,000 in 1990 to £1,830,000 in 1996.[6]

This investment in presentation in book-shops and in promotion appears to be paying off, with sales figures doubling from £948 million in 1985 to £1.7 billion in 1997.[7] Worpole notes that successful booksellers in the last decade have spent significant amounts in refitting their shops, taking account of modern retail expertise, conveying a clear brand image and not only responding to the market but 'creating new audiences and markets' and encouraging local managers to develop marketing activities within clear policy guidelines.[8]

It is necessary to clarify the difference between marketing and promotion since these two terms are often used interchangeably:

> *Marketing may be defined briefly as those activities that relate an organisation successfully to its environment. The main activities are the identification of unmet needs; the development of products and services to meet those needs, price, the distribution of goods to the marketplace and the communication of the ability of the products to meet those needs .[9]*

Promotion, as one of the four elements of the marketing mix, is concerned with communicating the benefits of the product to consumers and demonstrating how its qualities can meet their needs.

Baverstock provides an interpretation which is relevant to the book-trade:

> *it depends on the complete understanding of both product and designated market; an understanding that emerges only through detailed planning and research.*

In particular, she advocates knowledge of the product - i.e., the book - and how it relates to other books and to the consumer who may want that product and be prepared to pay for it 'once they have been informed of its existence'.[10]

The concept of applying marketing to the not-for-profit sector was developed in the Seventies, with Kotler and Andreasen, two of the earliest theorists to articulate how marketing could be applied to institutions such as hospitals, schools, universities and government. They identified the constraints of operating in organizations where political or budget restrictions, or professional ethics, may intercede and pointed out one of their greatest weaknesses, the lack of good secondary data about clients' behaviour patterns, perceptions, attitudes, likes and dislikes. They examined why it is more difficult to 'sell ideas or ideals than soap' and emphasized that the marketing manager's job is to influence demand and thus achieve organizational goals. This, if it is to succeed, must be customer-orientated but it does mean not trying to cater for every individual's wish. Segmentation and ensuring that a market segment is viable to meet organizational constraints is an essential part of successful marketing. Planning begins with the customer's wants and needs; these are then used to develop a strategic marketing plan which takes account of organizational resourcing constraints as well as objectives.[11]

Dragon clarifies how the marketing concept relates to library users. Substituting 'exchange' for 'pay' she states that market exchanges are value creating and should *'leave both parties with a sense of having gained something of value'*.[12] Value is however not being sufficiently generated according to some commentators - despite the high levels of satisfaction generally accorded to public libraries in satisfaction surveys, notably in MORI polls. Goodall accuses librarians of an 'anti-marketing strategy', with librarians restricting their buying to popular titles and argues for a more proactive approach if libraries are to survive.[13] Much of the effort in recent years in developing library services, though, has lain with the extension of information services and the targeting of disadvantaged groups. The sheer breadth of service offerings has made clear product definition and targeting of the fiction lending service, in the way that Goodall argues, more difficult.

In their study of strategic marketing in public libraries and leisure services, Kinnell and MacDougall found that a major problem lay with

> ...the long standing confusion over the definition of the role of services in local authorities. Should the emphasis for public libraries be on the educational role of encouragement to higher standards of literacy, wider reading habits, and adult education, or should resources be aimed at fulfilling the demand for popular recreational reading and audio visual materials?[14]

Before marketing concepts can be applied to the collections of leisure reading materials a library service has to answer such fundamental questions. Usually, public libraries attempt to be both educational and also broadly recreational/cultural organizations. There has to be some prioritizing, though, if finite resources are to be effectively deployed. Baker follows this reasoning in applying marketing principles to collection management: promotion should relate to mission, goals and objectives. Libraries which define target markets and closely specify the product and promotion and optimum frequency are likely to have the best results.[15]

Most of the literature relating to marketing in public libraries is concerned with marketing the service, particularly to the non-user, rather than marketing any of the libraries' specific products. Blocks to library promotion have been identified, specifically the lack of designated funding or staff responsibilities, material of less than professional standard and a lack of assessment of promotion against objectives.[16] However, there is evidence of considerable improvement in promotional materials as a whole in recent years and some influence of the Library Association/T.C.Farries award.[17] In order to develop the promotional role it is advocated that librarians should be promoters rather than curators, but there is concern to give libraries an overall positive profile by engaging in 'activities which may or may not be library or book related'.[18] The Audit Commission also asks for information on 'activities',[19] as does CIPFA but without requiring specific information on type or reasons for activities.

There is also disagreement at this non-specific approach, and reference to book trade practice for lessons on how to promote the library's product ;

> We have agonised over library promotion over the last decades; Waterstones does not promote Waterstones, it does not promote book -selling in general, it promotes what it offers ... by being bullish about our 'product' we would make far greater impact than trying to promote the public library in general.[20]

5.1.1 Developing public library reading promotion

As we discussed in Chapter 2, there was a distinct gap between statements about the significance of reading promotion and the planning for it. These findings generally accord with those of Kinnell and MacDougall, who found that public library services were well behind leisure services in their uses of marketing planning processes, although in 1994 only 4.31% of public library services had a marketing plan in place, with 14.38% 'in preparation',[21] so that there does appear to have been some progress, given that 18% of rspondents to this survey appeared to have a marketing/promotional plan in place. In order to further identify how reading promotion was developing, we asked library authorities to comment on a number of statements, as summarized in Table 12.

TABLE 12: *Reading promotion development*

STATEMENT	strongly agree %	neither strongly agree nor disagree %	strongly disagree %
Reading promotion is a core activity	90	9	0.7
To foster the reading habit should be a key task for librarians	92	8	0
Advising readers in their choice of books should be included in job descriptions of front line staff	65	27	6
Librarians underestimate the reading potential of the public	39	30	29
'The self effacing culture of librarians can lead to assumptions that librarians are ... without opinions or values of their own'. (Comedia Report)	47	26	25
We would make more impact by promoting recommended books than by promoting books/library services in general	35	32	32
It would be preferable for librarians to spend less time in selection and more in promotion	51	35	20
What we need is a national marketing agency similar to the Dutch NBLC	41	39	6

(It was interesting that 12% of authorities did not recognize the Dutch NBLC, a national library marketing and promotion agency.)

Some authorities sent copies of their plans, but some were just service plans which included an element of reading promotion, rather than a clearly defined reading promotion strategy as part of an overall marketing plan. One large municipal authority, under a service target to 'improve the quality of life', planned to:

- organize a readers' and writers' festival
- provide a full year programme for book exhibitions
- run six author events and develop six readers' and writers' groups
- improve the quality of library promotions and displays through training.

In some cases, it was difficult to identify reading promotion within service plans which were either building-based, client-focused, e.g., special services, children and young people, or service- provision orientated, i.e., reference and information services or specific area or library targets. In other cases it was difficult to identify exactly what was planned. Some action plans appeared to be more policy than action.

One authority felt the concentration had been on general promotion:

we are not sufficiently focused compared with general promotion of the service.

Another respondent admitted:

I don't feel we have concentrated on reading promotion here. I would like to change this as I feel this is more important than other promotions we do .

(Senior Librarian, London Borough)

This authority, which has a promotions policy, states in a policy document on promotions that before planning any kind of promotion it is necessary to establish clear aims and desired outcomes. It lists twelve possible aims for a promotion including advertising a new service, increasing awareness of current or topical issues, forging links with other organizations as well as exploiting literature to raise awareness and improve performance of specific areas of stock.

Another is to some extent redefining the service by focusing on reading for pleasure, to ensure that, under a new structure, the library is not subsumed in the Education Department's objectives:

We don't want to lose the pleasure element in reading.

(Chief Librarian, London Borough)

Their definition of reading for pleasure includes non-fiction such as popular science and popular psychology. There are short term and long term plans which link stock purchase, display, cataloguing, indexing and categorization, staff training and a strategy forum to plan and implement new ideas for promotional work, making use of information gained from public feedback. A policy statement which was initiated by a grass roots working group also ensured that this was a staff development exercise.

Only one authority produced a specific marketing plan for book promotion: for a countywide year-long promotion with sections on aims, product, image, target markets, promotional activities, materials, resources, action plan and evaluation. The target group included adults and young people. The overall theme was 'Books for all Seasons' and the plan took a monthly changing theme incorporating fiction and non fiction topics, including armchair travel, parks and gardens and, for Christmas, books to give and receive. Events to tie in with the themes included those co-ordinated at county level and others arranged locally. A newsletter on similar lines to that used by the book retail chains served to ensure good communication and staff motivation.

5.2 From displays and events to promotions

We asked authorities about their programmes of reading promotion activities, in order to assess the range and extent of promotional activity. Even although much of this was not part of a marketing plan for reading development, there was evidence of substantial work in progress :

TABLE 13: *Reading promotion initiatives*

INITIATIVE	%
preparation of booklists/reading guides	78
programme of author visits	77
circulating displays	68
competitions	59
literature festival	42
other	27

Although we stated in the questionnaire that our survey only related to reading promotion for adults some authorities did include children's activities. Unless promotions were intended to be for all ages we have excluded these from the findings. The figure for competitions, in particular, may be misleading.

In interviews and comments from the questionnaires we found that despite the lack of formal planning resourcing limitations had forced library services to consider their promotional programmes and to target resources more carefully. Defining what was to be achieved was seen to be important:

> *We are changing the focus from the number of displays produced to what's displayed: redefining the blanket term , to use activities instead of promotions.*
> (Principal Libraries Officer, Metropolitan District)

> *We're now focusing on reading rather than writing as literature development officers have done in the past!*

Coherent programmes were especially successful. 'Traveller's tales: a festival of journeys' was an imaginative week- long promotion which was held in different parts of a rural county. It featured displays on walking, explorers, a taste of abroad and the art of the travel writer. There were events to tie in - 'Meet the travellers and hear their tales' - but the focus was on reading and books rather than on writing and authors.

There is a number of examples of multi-faceted promotions but, again, a coherent set of objectives was seen to be important in order to fulfil quite wide-ranging (too wide?) expectations:

'Future fantastic' was devised

> *to provide reading guidance to the public; to provide a corporate image for promotional activities; to promote reading and literacy to all ages; to co-ordinate sponsorship; to promote arts events*
> (Planning Document, County authority)

This package of county wide and local events and promotions on the theme of fantasy and the future will include author visits, book-lists, sound recordings lists, story-telling, poetry and a reading game. The promotion will be run over the whole county for a six- month period.

5.2.1 Displays

We found that 68% of libraries had organized circulating displays, with varying emphasis on this in their promotional programmes. One authority has moved away from writer events as the main thrust of its book promotion programme and turned towards reader- centred promotion *'A scheme which offered the public the chance to meet writers, had little or no impact on library use'*. The focus was changed and, whilst a writers' programme was retained, an equal share of resources was put into creating quality displays supported by booklists and careful selections of books, and these have been effective. The author events were successful in gaining people from outside the locality; in contrast the displays attracted regular users who:

> *are willing to take the risk of reading poetry or Asian fiction but unwilling to turn up for a special event.*

(Area Manager, County Borough).

A number of experiments has shown that issues of particular titles increased significantly when books were displayed in highly visible and accessible locations (prime location sites). A research project which sought to establish whether this was because of increased accessibility or 'information overload' concluded that increased accessibility is the major factor in encouraging use. A wide range of stock could be issued in this way rather than just popular or new titles. Where displays are 'fixed' rather than at 'point of sale' they need to be changed frequently and where this is not feasible rotating displays should be provided.[22] Goldhor came to similar conclusions[23] and Hermenze describes a successful experiment in promoting the use of classics by inviting library users to contribute to a permanent display of books which had 'changed lives or stirred imaginations'.[24]

5.2.2 Bibliographies

Bibliographies for public use were available in 94% of libraries. There is a tendency for readers to look for a specific author, the reader seeking not only genre but particular treatment or style. This was the stimulus for the launch of the 'who else writes like' guide,[25] which as we noted in Chapter

1 now guides the user through 1,084 authors with the names of alternative novelists.[26] A survey conducted by the Library and Information Statistics Unit indicated a range of fiction guides and showed differences in authorities' attitudes to making these available for public use. For instance, the *Bloomsbury Guide to fiction authors* was available in 41% of authorities but only readily accessible to the public in 30% of these.[27]

5.2.3 Posters, lists, bookmarks and publications

We found that 78% of libraries were involved in the preparation of booklists, although the evidence on the effectiveness of these kinds of promotional aids is mixed. Goodall found 18%of her respondents had used posters to help them find books[28] and Spiller found that 76% of his interviewees stated they would make use of booklists when these were available[29] but he warned that this was the type of subjective question which tended to bring out a positive response. Jennings and Sear found 80% of their users did not use bookmarks, which 85% had not even noticed, while 60% of these said they would try them after being alerted to their existence. Even 'allowing for the politeness factor' they concluded that bookmarks appear worthwhile and would be welcomed by readers.[30]

One view is that booklists 'help alleviate overload' but that they will only be effective if widely distributed and easily found amongst all the other stimuli competing for attention. They need to be assertively promoted.[31] Goldhor found that *'titles placed in a booklist increase their circulation by a factor of four whereas titles placed on a display increase circulation by seven,'* explaining this by the reader effort involved.[32] There is also the potential for a booklist to link works not brought together by classification or catalogues. It is suggested that librarians need to relax their mental prohibition against linking fiction and non fiction, and should write reviews which trap on paper *'that elusive spirit that makes it appeal to readers'.*[33]

We also asked whether library services had worked on adult reading promotion in collaboration with other organizations and agencies. A number of library authorities are now working in consortia with regional arts or library supplier support, producing linked poster/booklist packages.

It was interesting here that one or two authorities which were part of a consortium working with a library supplier indicated that they felt that the cessation of the net book agreement (NBA) meant that such joint working was in the favour of library suppliers. Combined spending power and the fact that libraries were willing to spearhead promotion initiatives meant that suppliers could capitalise, and use these initiatives with their other customers. On the other hand the manager of one library supplier indicated that with the close margins since NBA there was no way they could continue to provide this support. Another supplier stated that it was only possible to offer a measured discount from a menu of services which included promotions. Libraries should not expect to get maximum discount and additional services and there was a strong danger of losing them unless libraries were realistic.

TABLE 14: *Joint promotions*

	%
other library services	20
library suppliers	29
local bookshops	19
regional arts board	34
other	34

Well Worth Reading is the best known example of this type of initiative. Begun in 1987, following criticisms by Southern Arts of a lack of library promotion, a pilot project was launched to *'stimulate through libraries the supply and demand for good contemporary fiction'*. The consortium originally comprised Southern Arts and Dorset, Berkshire and Hampshire libraries. Direct Contact, a marketing firm, was appointed as co-ordinator to develop a series of themed promotional booklists with reviews and co-ordinated posters. Southern Arts took a qualitative stance from the start of the project: its aim to encourage libraries to purchase good books by proving demand. Evaluation showed that overall a title was likely to be borrowed twice as much if included in a Well Worth Reading promotion After the initial phase it was necessary to gain sponsorship from the commercial sector, which has been obtained from a number of library suppliers. In 1990, Dorset, West Sussex and Hampshire supported by Southern and South West Arts, and a library supplier, with Miranda McKearney, an independent consultant, as co-ordinator, took the project further into a new self-financing phase. Promotions which are initiated by librarians in the three authorities focus on contemporary fiction under themes such as 'Body and Soul' 'Obsessions' or 'Turning Points' using leaflets, bookmarks and posters. Over 70 library authorities have used the promotion. In 1995, a series of general themed posters was launched to enable librarians to exploit the stock of any library. A key factor of the scheme has been the amount of experimentation, with changing partnerships and evolving criteria.[34]

Future expansion could include a programme of authors touring, dump-bins, use of multi-media and reader participation and in 1998 more changes are planned. 'A right laugh', a humour promotion, and a major poetry promotion will involve external training by Opening the Book consultants.

A Right Good Read is a fiction promotion scheme subscribed to by Yorkshire Arts and Wakefield, Bradford, Calderdale, Kirklees and Doncaster. Begun in 1990, it continues to provide a means of vigorously promoting fiction to library users, enhancing the public profile and enhancing staff skills. Evaluation has shown positive user response. Whilst librarians are finding the scheme a great success, successive promotions have demonstrated the importance of display. Subjects have included 'Great villains,' 'Underfire' 'Great romances' and 'The great American novel.'

Now Read On started in Scotland in November, 1991, as a joint promotion by the Scottish Arts Council and the Scottish Library Association and *'was intended to give library readers some guidance through the maze of contemporary quality fiction'*. It provides themed bi-monthly displays, booklists, posters, dump-bins, all produced to professional standard. Used by 32 of the then 42 library authorities, evaluation shows a uniform level of take- up in both rural and city areas. The project prompted a seminar in Glasgow in 1993 and since then has led to authorities looking critically at book selection policies. It is said to have produced a 329% increase in issues.[35] In 1993 Book Trust Scotland was brought into the team who took over the management of the project and the latest promotion in August, 1995 was judged the most successful. After a lull caused by local government reorganization, a further promotion is due in 1997, subject to funding.

'Breaking barriers', book promotions currently touring Liverpool libraries, are based on the premise that

> *many library users are looking for a good read, but are unsure of what to try. A thematic approach is used to encourage riskier reading by including a selection of books that include popular and more serious reading.*
>
> (Explanatory document concerning this service.)

The promotions tour most libraries in the city, spending four weeks in any library. Evaluation shows that they have been successful in stimulating issues, encouraging riskier reading. They are also sold to other libraries as promotion packages.

Multi-Story Building started in 1996 as an East of England library forum promotion, the participants being the East of England Regional Arts Board and libraries in Bedfordshire and Cambridgeshire, Essex,

Hertfordshire, Lincolnshire, Norfolk and Suffolk. In addition to its supply of booklists, each library receives a table-top dispenser. The promotion is part of a festival with two performers touring the region.

The Seals project was officially launched in May, 1993. The first 12 collections each consisting of 300 novels in French, German, Italian and Spanish went out to 11 libraries in the West Midlands. A printed catalogue which featured 3000 titles, recommended by continental library colleagues, contains background information on authors and genres. Since the project began stock has been issuing at an increase of 150%. An article on the project concluded:

> Now that European issues are more and more on the agenda, public libraries should be in the forefront of encouraging reading in other languages for those who need or want it. Is there a wider lesson here which UK and Ireland librarians could apply to other specialist areas too?[36]

The East Midlands Arts Region also felt a need to respond to Europe by entering into a partnership with Ireland and Holland to organize an international conference. The proceedings include an account of the Dutch NBLC, a national umbrella organization which promotes collective interests and provides products, services, systems and furnishings. Holland has a national reviewing and centralised ordering scheme.[37] A further example, The Danish Library Bureau, Biblitekcentralen, was established in 1937. Although the idea of a central support agency had been considered previously it was not until a decision was made to hold back 2.5 % of the total state grant for the provision of common services, that the idea came to fruition.[38] The idea of a similar national marketing agency for Britain has been mooted for some years. In 1981, Cronin argued for one and explored a number of different models, concluding that a combination of American and German practice should be commended.[39]

A formal proposal for a centralised marketing agency for Britain was finally made in 1996 by Miranda McKearney. The rationale was that libraries have had a fragmented approach to marketing, and a centralised agency is needed on grounds of cost-effectiveness and quality of production. The proposal was for a study into the feasibility of a national marketing agency for publicly funded libraries. This would include information exchange, fund raising, PR, research, networking, focus development, local programming, merchandising and brokering. The suggested research would identify professional credibility, attitudes, methodology, etc. This proposal, which has been supported by the Library Association, has recently been repackaged to form the basis of a bid for national lottery money to meet the Arts for Everyone criteria, with additional interest and support from, among others, the Society of Chief Librarians. Possible areas for inclusion are: staff development and training the trainers, mapping or gathering information on key players and relationships and regional networks.

5.2.4 Literature festivals

We found that 42% of respondents had run a literature festival. Much of this type of initiative has come about as a result of Arts Council funding; often it has been undertaken with the help of literature development workers and with the support of Regional Arts Boards.

According to one literature development worker, the aim from the Arts Council is not only publicising new writers or new work and encouraging readers and writing but *'bridging the gap between readers and writers'*. The organizers of 'Opening the book', the first Sheffield literature festival, saw both the dangers and the opportunities of these initiatives:

> *too often a festival is short term excitement, underfunded, reliant on volunteers and leaves in its wake a trail of disappointment and frustration.*

They decided to organize a festival which would

> *demystify the processes involving the written word and the reader, examining the role of the literary establishment and its relation to borrowers and writers, explore the potential of libraries to intervene in the debates about reading and writing...and above all make any reader feel confident about what they read and how they read - and from that basis tempt them to try something new* .[40]

Another festival, 'Off the shelf', has been running for a number of years. The week-long festival for 1996, called 'Flights of fancy,' had imaginatively devised events which included a writers' workshop, a chance to meet regional publishers, literary lunches, tea with Jane Austen at the museum and a 'Magical mystery tour - a coach journey with a difference'.

'Getting into poetry' was a poetry festival which according to the organizers boosted loans of modern poetry and inspired staff to experiment in developing poetry stock, with over 600 people attending 11 events.

> *We were locked into the familiar cycle of low issues leading to a reluctance to buy new stock leading to ever lower public expectations. So we invited modern poets to help ... the enthusiasm of the poets was infectious and they demonstrated to staff that what they write can be extremely relevant of everyday life.*
>
> (Bradford Library Service evaluation of 'Getting into poetry')

5.2.5 Author events

The majority, 76%, of our respondents had organised author events, which are a less ambitious way of bringing authors and readers together than a full-blown festival. Some authorities are seeking ways of improving the interaction between writers and readers.
'Dialogue' will encourage:

> *conversations between writers and reader, library staff and the public. By conversations we mean a programme of stimulating activities that encourages what is usually a one way private exchange*

> *(Metropolitan Borough).*

Davidson recommends setting a target audience for any event

> *To expect fifty or a hundred for a well known crime writer is not unreasonable. To expect twenty for a little known poet is just as reasonable, provided you are happy to take on the work for the level of audience .*[41]

'Write On' was one such programme that grew out of a perceived demand for creative writing opportunities:

> *'It offered the public a chance to meet writers and find out more about their work by providing programmes featuring national celebrities and writers from the rich pool of local talent. There was a large element of audience participation through lively question and answer sessions and performance opportunities for would be writers ...*
> (City Library Service - Information provided with Questionnaire)

5.2.6 Book discussion groups

One authority which has a post of reader-in-residence has put at the top of a list of priorities for development:

> *Working with the community amongst users and non users of the library service: to set up and run an initial 10 week course looking at contemporary fiction with the intention of leading this into monthly reading groups with additional related activities.*

Reading groups where readers can share their interest and pleasure in what is usually a solitary pursuit appear to have become popular. Van Riel, commenting on reader behaviour, refers to Jean Binta Breeze who is said to want every reader to have a different journey when they read her work.

> *'This is why talking about reading is exciting and interesting. Someone else's interpretation could be significantly different from yours. An exchange of information can shed light on what you might have already read and can introduce you to new possibilities for what to read next'.*[42]

Opening the book: finding a good read, discussed in Chapter 1, is the result of such conversations with readers sharing their enthusiasms. It gives readers an opportunity to analyse their reading personality, explains the 'risks' associated with making a choice: books may be difficult to start or boring, upsetting, difficult to understand etc., then takes the reader on a series of reading journeys, building bridges between different types of genre.[43]

Recently, Waterstones have produced literature on how to start a reading group backed with a series of 'Vintage reading guides' for specific books, the initiative largely stemming from the USA, where reading groups are becoming well known.

5.2.7 Reader-centred promotion

Watson notes that the arts funding system has clearly provided a catalyst but states that it would be wrong to place too much emphasis on this, arguing that *'a gradual metamorphosis has come about in the rationale of local authorities'*. He argues that we have come from the nineteenthcentury paternalism through a time when the *'ethic of post war librarianship, was providing the public with what they wanted without making any distinction between good or bad.'* With the growth and diversification of mass culture and the sheer volume of printed material now produced people now need help in making choices: *'with all this choice does anyone know what they want anymore?.*[44]

Certainly, Van Riel feels that *'a major strength of the library service is its non- judgmental attitude'* but she also argues that little is done for the majority of users who are not sure of what they want to read and states that 50% of all issues have been shown to come from the 'returns trolley'. *'A tiny proportion of stock is working to tremendous capacity whilst acres of books lie untouched on the shelves'.*

> Opening the book now uses the term 'reader development', this recognises different needs, acknowledges the subjectivity of the reading experience and is proactive in widening choice and access. It offers a middle way and avoids a clash between the neutrality of the library profession and the commitment of the Arts Council to literature.

One of their practical and simple suggestions is to make use of this fact by, for example, labelling the returns trolley with headlines like 'Other readers suggest' and to encourage interaction between reader and reader, and reader and library staff, through reader reviews on notice boards, linking readers with specific interests, organizing book discussion groups, and so forth.[45]

'Reading between the lines' is an attempt by one authority to encourage readers to comment on books they have read. A simple slip is available for readers with the request 'Tell us about what you are reading, what did you like most, or least about this book?' Readers are asked to state if they *don't* want their review to be used to promote books with other readers. The response has been good, one member of staff comments:

> We got a lot of feedback, individual written responses to books some favourable some honestly critical; 98% of people go in and out of libraries with little comment, some complain and with this suddenly we were getting a response, it was wonderful.
>
> (Team Leader, County Library service)

Another authority has a similar scheme, readers are encouraged to share their reading in *Bookstraps,* a monthly free magazine which is also used to publicise literature and reading promotion events and activities.

Another authority is using its reading groups to produce 'Novel approach: living writers from around the world read and reviewed by staff and users'.

A municipal borough is linking its readers through 'Reading chains' enabling them to share experience through a library notice board.

More than one authority has sought to widen readers' taste by lending surprise packages. One promotion entitled 'Lazy days' comprised a sealed paper bag with two paper back books for holiday reading, a tourist guide, a film processing envelope and a prize draw form for a weekend at a luxury hotel. The scheme ran from June - August and 5000 bags were issued, with very positive feedback.

Another authority organized a reading trail 'Going for gold' - tied in with the Olympic games. Using the terminology of the games, short stories were re-titled 'Sprint events' and white melamine guides in the shelving guided readers round a novel-reading trail. The same authority organized a 'day of reading' with a wall of reviews, borrowed armchairs with people reading and a specially orchestrated event during which local babies joined the library.

5.3 Promoting non-fiction

Despite the acceptance that popular non-fiction had an important role to play in leisure reading and the widening of experience we found disappointingly little promotion of non- fiction. In support of this need we found in an advertisement for a Head of Reader Services one authority stating its belief that:

> Literature covers many genres, including contemporary fiction, classics, biography, travel and seeks to be defined by the user and not by the convenience of the librarian.
>
> (City Library and Information Service - job advertisement)

However, there were interesting examples:

1. One service produced some imaginative booklists: 'Homage to Spain' and 'The French Collection' were both designed to support language learning classes. The French booklist includes philosophy, arts, food and wine, travel, novels, fiction in translation, living and working, biography and history. It is available on the Internet, together with information about the classes.
2. 'Wordpower' was produced as part of a programme entitled 'Influences' to celebrate the 1995 UK Year of Literature: *a sample menu from which to explore the varied flavours of the literary and musical cultures of our neighbours'.*
3. A science fiction festival which incorporated informational programmes about astronomy, etc., was designed to appeal to all ages.
4. Durham's literature festival for 1996 celebrated the visual arts and included exhibitions of William Morris and 'Why don't we understand contemporary art?

But, on the whole the majority of promotions were for fiction and there was comparatively little material which crossed the boundaries or sought to pull together different sections of the classification to exploit the whole stock of library materials.

5.4 Presentation and arrangement

Promotion is much more than activity. One of the obvious successes of the book world lies in the ambience created in bookshops - the way in which the look of bookshops has changed to make stock more accessible and to let the books sell themselves by front-on or table- top display. Libraries have made several attempts to achieve equally successful shelving and 'atmospherics'.

Alternative shelf arrangements have been used in libraries since the 1930s, Detroit being one of the first library services to develop such a system.[46] Prior to 1965 Tottenham were about to move towards 'reader centred arrangement', a broad series of groups based on use and interest rather than subjects.[47] But the main interest in alternative arrangements in public libraries came in the 1970s. Ainley and Totterdell describe approaches and methods of presentation in a number of library authorities. They summarise the reasons as: a move towards user orientation; financial problems forcing public libraries to maximise their resources; reduced book funds causing libraries to rethink the idea of a 'balanced stock' and look for a 'closer fit between supply and demand'.[48] Various user studies are cited which they consider show that a minority of users are seeking specific authors or titles: the majority are browsers.

Miller describes a new look for Glasgow libraries *'in the face of multiplying detractions, public layout is a factor in promotion of library use'*.[49]

One London Borough has taken presentation and arrangement as its first priority in promoting reading 't*he bulk of the stock is still on ordinary shelves but the shelves are now standard book-shop type and take book-shop guiding'*.[50] Categorization is used and also dump-bins and 'Splashbins' - selections of new books before allocation to the home library. This authority is no longer using suppliers' dump-bins and has commissioned its own - *'up to now we've been dependent on suppliers but now we are leading ourselves'*. Considerable effort has gone into a readers' questionnaire which asks readers to state what they were looking for and to indicate how useful the new arrangement is:

- 76% of readers think the traditional method of display encourages looking for known authors.
- 79% thought displays encourage borrowing new authors
- 96% did not come intending to find a title.

Thus development was*:*

> part of an overall policy where it was decided that spending less on stock and more on staff and ambience would give results. The committee allowed six months to prove the changes in six libraries. The results were conclusive.
>
> (Assistant Director, London Borough.)

In the questionnaire, we asked about library layout and other facilities designed to assist readers in their choice of books and we also asked library authorities to state which options they felt were most effective.

TABLE 15: *Library layout*

FACILITIES AVAILABLE	%
face on display	97
catergorisation	82
dumpbins	69
guiding as a section aid	67
printed bibliographical tools for public use	66
laid out browsing area	37
annotated OPAC	20
Hypertext/CD-ROM selection aids	12

Of the wide range of different layouts being used,those ranked most important were :

1.face- on display
2.guiding
3.categorization

5.4.1 Browsing

There is considerable evidence that the serendipitous user has not been accorded enough consideration by libraries. Traditional arrangements and catalogues do not suit readers' behaviour in libraries: behaviour well understood by bookshops.

Sear and Jennings pointed out the need to take account of user behaviour, particularly in the selection of fiction. They found that the majority of readers in Kent selected by browsing and that 85% of books chosen this way were by authors new to the reader, with 52% who had looked for known authors being disappointed. The most popular reason for deciding on a book was the blurb; 20% of readers were looking for a specific genre, one-third admitted difficulty in choosing. Where the reader knew something about author or title four out of five books were enjoyed but where the book was selected by browsing only one third were satisfied. They concluded that the most popular method of selecting appeared to have the poorest user satisfaction rates and that more should be done to help the browser.[51]

They went on to set up a browsing area at Severn Oaks library with books arranged under themes, chosen as a means of stimulating the process of choosing. Readers using the browsing area liked discovering new authors, were less daunted by the volume of choice; where themes corresponded with their interests it was a time-saver and whereas in the first survey only 33% enjoyed books chosen this way the figure was now increased to 56%.[52]

An earlier study of fiction borrowing patterns in four library services had also drawn attention to the importance of browsing, revealing that the major reason people selected by browsing was because they lacked information on what to look for, or were unable to remember titles or authors, though some people liked the freedom associated with browsing.[53] These findings were reinforced by a study of the readership of literary fiction[54] and by Goodall's study which found that only one-third of books were taken from the alphabetical sequence, the rest from other sequences and that the overwhelming majority of readers (87%) never use the catalogue.[55]

Research in Sydney, Australia, which looked at both fiction and non-fiction showed that 50% of users admitted that they usually came to the library to browse, 36% to browse generally, the remainder to browse specifically, i.e., in subject area/s. It was found that users were unhappy with over-full shelves, they liked collections they could relate to, such as books on TV or film and they found librarians too busy supplying information to give help in finding interesting reading. There is a plea for simple arrangements and floor- walking readers' advisors.[56]

5.4.2 Categorization

We were therefore interested to see how far libraries were meeting these needs and adopting commercial practices. Alternative arrangements have made use of shop-type shelving with more emphasis on guiding and front- on display, but the main emphasis has been on categorization.The majority of libraries have confined categorization to fiction, although there are a few examples of libraries which have categorized all stock.[57] Genre classification is particularly popular in the USA. In one study, 96% of the 47 libraries surveyed used this method, although there were compatabilities with only three categories: science fiction, westerns and mysteries and widely different views on the rest.[58]

A study of a range of schemes found that there was no one recognized fiction scheme available nor was consistent analysis possible, but it was concluded that if categorization increased access then this was not a matter of major concern. Three methods were noted: spine labelling of books in normal sequence, separating categories and placing in a separate area, and an amalgamation of both.[59] Information overload in American libraries has been identified as a major issue, and an investigation of the effects of classification and categorization in libraries of different sizes found that the larger the library the more it is needed.[60] Despite these advantages of categorization, criticisms have been made at the dispersing of authors, the non-exclusiveness of schemes and at 'encouraging laziness'.[61] There is clearly general agreement in the literature, however, that in order to manage fiction appropriately in libraries, methods which are in harmony with user behaviour are essential.[62] The success of book shops in applying market buyer behaviour to their merchandising ought to be emulated.

It was therefore interesting to note that 82% of our respondents categorized their libraries to some degree. However, one library supplier identified as a major disadvantage the very large numbers of categories some authorities are using and the almost complete variation in library authorities' selection of categories and symbols. There was an urgent need for nationally agreed standards.

5.4.3 Classification schemes for fiction

Fiction has largely been ignored in major classification schemes, so that a considerable number of studies have focused on this issue.[63] Beghtol[64] and Pejtersen[65] have both tried to produce a multi-dimensional system of fiction classification. Beghtol provides four main elements (characters, events spaces and time), joined by expressive notation which seeks toidentify relationships. Pejtersen has *'made the most important contribution, bringing fiction into the territory of modern information retrieval'.*[66] This work identified the importance of readers being enabled to formulate their needs and, based on observation and analysis of the interaction between reader and librarian, found that readers tend to explain their needs by subject frame or setting in time or place, the theme or emotions or ideas and accessibility or style or language or writing. The AMP classification scheme (analysis and mediation of publications) uses four 'dimensions': subject matter and frame, author's intention, style, and readability. The scheme, which has seldom been implemented, would require readers to be precise and articulate in their requests, and be demanding of library staff time, but it is argued it would help librarians to know their stock better.[67]

A new British Library cataloguing initiative *'seeks to redress the imbalance between the level of access provided for fiction and non fiction'.*[68] From January 1997 British National Bibliography catalogue records are being indexed using Library of Congress headings in conjunction with a range of genre and form headings derived from the American Library Association Guidelines on subject access to individual works of fiction. These will show form/genre, characters, setting and topic.

5.4.4 Information technology

Research has shown minimal use of library catalogues for the selection of reading for pleasure. Goodall's finding that 87% of users never access the catalogue was replicated in the Kent survey where 86% was the figure.[69] Use of a computerised database can give different points of access and if linked to an on-line issue system could obviate the frustration of finding a reference to a book taken out by another reader. Pejtersen's Bookhouse is an icon based system of retrieval used on a mobile library to achieve this.[70] Betts has suggested that computers could be used for self service selection by keyword searching and matched with reader profiles to provide a high level of personalised service.[71]

When investigating how far public libraries had begun to implement technological solutions to retrieval, we found that 20% of library services had annotated OPACs and 17% had Hypertext/CDROM selection aids. Clearly, there was scope for development. CD-ROM, although considered relatively old technology, is providing a new means of information access for users. Currently used by suppliers as an alternative or in addition to approval collections it provides a user friendly record which gives, in addition to author and title, the blurb, a two-page spread including colour illustrations and reviews.

The Internet is already being used as an interactive review mechanism with scope for lists and comments by readers. One authority made Web pages available for reader recommendations, seeded by staff, but found that the respondents came from places as far away as from Southern California. Other authorities are putting onto the Web recommended titles, lists of literary prizes, etc. A library service in the West Midlands has made the facility available for local authors to give brief details of their current work. The West Midlands Regional Library Bureau has recently launched its Lit Net

> *which will contain listings of readers and writers groups, what's on, links to other sites and an on- line forum for site visitors to interact with one another.*
>
> (Press release for Lit Net)

IT presents a rapidly expanding field with considerable potential for use in sharing ideas.

5.5 Summary

There was evidence of a range of initiatives in progress, with collaborative programmes offering valuable examples of good practice. It was also evident, though, that libraries were not exploiting their book stocks sufficiently through more effective shelving arrangements and the use of creative merchandising techniques. Categorization had been widely implemented, but there was huge scope for use of information retrieval techniques and the Internet to inform and involve readers. A great deal is now known about user borrowing behaviour, and it was seen as vital that libraries emulate the book trade in exploiting this kind of knowledge to ensure greater participation by their communities.

References

1. COMEDIA. *Borrowed time? The future of public libraries in the United Kingdom.* Stroud: Comedia, 1993, 65.

2. PHELAN, K. *Libraries and reading promotion schemes. Working paper 5.* Stroud: Comedia, 1993, 3.

3. BAVERSTOCK, A. *Are books different? Marketing and the book trade.* London: Kegan Paul, 1993.

4. BAVERSTOCK, A. *How to market books.* London: Kegan Paul, 1993.

5. BOOK MARKETING LTD. *Books and the consumer.* London: Book Marketing Ltd. Published annually.

6. BOOK MARKETING LTD. *Bookfacts.* London: Book Marketing Ltd, 1996, 7

7. *Cultural Trends*, March, 1997.

8. WORPOLE, K. *The public library and the bookshop. Working paper 3.* Stroud: Comedia, 1993.

9. HUGHES, G. D. *Marketing management: a planning approach.* London: Addison Wesley, 1978, 3.

10. BAVERSTOCK. *How to market books, op cit,* 34.

11. KOTLER, P and A. ANDREASEN. *Strategic marketing for non-profit organizations.* Englewood Cliffs, N.J.: Prentice Hall, 1987.12.Dragon, A. C. The marketing of public library services. *Drexel Library Quarterly,* 19 (2) 1983,118

13. GOODALL, D. *Browsing in public libraries.* Loughborough: Loughborough University Library and Information statistics Unit, 1989.

14. KINNELL, M. and J. MACDOUGALL. *Meeting the marketing challenge:strategies for public libraries and leisure services.* London: Taylor Graham, 1994, 114.

15. BAKER, S. L. *The responsive public library collection.* Englewood, Col: Libraries Unlimited, 1993.

16. WOODHOUSE, R. G. and J. NEILL. *The promotion of public library use.* London: British Library, 1978 (Research and Development Report 5470).

17. PYLE, J. Publicity and promotion. In: *British librarianship and information work 1986 - 1990. Vol 1.General libraries and the profession.* London: Library Association Publishing, 1992, 199 - 207.

18. KING, I. *Promote: the handbook of public library promotion.* London: Public Libraries Group of the Library Association, 1986.

19. AUDIT COMMISSION FOR LOCAL GOVERNMENT IN ENGLAND AND WALES. *Performance review in local government: leisure and libraries.* London: HMSO, 1986.

20. WALTERS, R. The library, the bookshop and the literature centre. *New Library World,* 1116, 1996, 25.

21. KINNELL and MACDOUGALL, *op. cit,* 64-65.

22. BAKER, S. L. Why book displays increase use: a review of causal factors. *Public Libraries,* Summer, 1986, 63-65

23. GOLDHOR, H. The effect of prime display location on public library circulation of selected adult titles. *Library Quarterly,* 42 (4), 1972, 371-389.

24. HERMENZE, J. The classics will circulate. *Library Journal,* Nov 15, 1981, 2192-2195.

25. MANN, P. H. *The readers' guide to fiction authors.* Loughborough: Loughborough University Library and Information Statistics Unit, 1985.

26. HUSE, R. and J. HUSE. *Who else writes like? A reader's guide to fiction authors.* Loughborough: Loughborough University Library and Information Statistics Unit, 1996.

27. MARRIOTT, R. How well do libraries inform their public? *Library Association Record,* 95 March, 1993, 164-167.

28. GOODALL, *op cit.*

29. SPILLER, D. The provision of fiction in public libraries. *Journal of Librarianship,* 12 (4) 1980, 226-38.

30. JENNINGS and SEAR, *op cit.*

31. BAKER, S. *The responsive public library collection, op cit,* 267.

32. GOLDHOR, *op cit.*

33. BAKER, S. L. Booklists: what we know, what we need to know. *R.Q.,* Winter, 1993, 178180.

34. MCKEARNEY, M. Well worth reading: fiction scheme comes of age. *Public Library Journal,* 5(3), 1990 61 -2.

35. PHELAN, *op cit*, 7.

36. WARREN, G. Reading across Europe. *Public Library Journal*, 11(4), 1996, 97-100.

37. TIEBOLT, M. A national strategy for marketing and promoting literature in libraries. In: Tasker, J. and J. Shepherd, eds. *Words across Europe partnership. Report and recommendations*. Northampton: Northamptonshire County Council, 1997.

38. ALSTER, L. Bibliotekscentraleni. The Danish Library Bureau. *Scandinavian Public Libraries Quarterly*, 1(4), 1968, 226-238.

39. CRONIN, B. Nationally co-ordinated library provision. *Journal of Librarianship*, 13, 1981, 221- 230.

40. *Opening the book: a report to the Arts Council*. London: The Arts Council, 1989.

41. DAVIDSON, J. Planning and running library events. In: Stewart, I. *Shelf talk*. London: Arts Council of England, 1996.

42. VAN RIEL, R. *Reader centred promotion*. In: Stewart, I. *Shelf talk*. London: Arts Council of England, 1996, 1.16.

43. VAN RIEL, R. *and* O. FOWLER. *Opening the book: finding a good read*. Bradford: Bradford Libraries, 1996.

44. WATSON, D. Empowering literary choice. *Library Association Record*, 98(9), 1996, 462-465.45.Van Riel, R. Why promote?. In: Stewart, I. *Shelf talk*. London: Arts Council of England, 1996, 1, 1.01, 1.02.

46. DETROIT PUBLIC LIBRARY. *The reader interest arrangement in Detroit Public Library*. Detroit: Detroit Public Library, 1959.

47. DUNKLIN, P. E. Some aspects of stock provision: Tottenham Public Libraries. In: Association of Assisitant Librarians. *Some aspects of stock provision*. London: Association of Assistant Librarians, 1964.

48. AINLEY, P. *and* B. TOTTERDELL. *Alternative arrangements: new approaches to public library stock*. London: Association of Assistant Librarians, 1982.

49. MILLER, A. Alternative arrangements in Glasgow central library. *Public Library Journal*, 7(5), 1992, 19.

50. LONDON BOROUGH OF BROMLEY LEISURE SERVICES DEPARTMENT. Unpublished papers, 1990 onwards.

51. JENNINGS, B. *and* L. SEAR. How readers select fiction: a survey in Kent. *Public Libraries Journal*, 1(4), 1986, 43-7.

52. JENNINGS, B. *and* L. SEAR. Novel ideas. A browsing area for fiction. *Public Libraries Journal*, 4(3), 1989, 41-44

53. SPILLER, *op.* cit.

54. SPENCELEY, N. The readership of literary fiction; a survey of library users in the Sheffield area. MA dissertation. Sheffield University, Department of Information Studies, 1989.

55. GOODALL, *op cit.*

56. WILLARD, P. *and* V. B. TEECE. The browser and the library. *Public Libraries Quarterly*, (Sydney, Australia) 1983, 55- 63.

57. AINLEY *and* TOTTERDELL, *op cit.*

58. HARRELL, G. *and* E. G. HARRELL. The classification and organization of adult fiction in large American public libraries. *Public Libraries* 24, Spring, 13-14 .

59. CORNS, I. J. A study into fiction classification and cataloguing. M.A. dissertation. Loughborough University Department of Information and Library Studies, 1995.

60. BAKER, S. L. Will fiction classification schemes increase use? *R. Q.*, 3, 1988, 366-376.

61. DIXON. J. *Fiction in libraries*. London: Library Association, 1986.

62. KINNELL, M., ed. *Managing fiction in libraries*. London: Library Association Publishing, 1991.

63. YU, L. *and* A. O'BRIEN. Domain of adult fiction librarianship. *Advances in Librarianship*, 20, 1986, 167.

64. BEGHTOL, C. *The classification of fiction*. Metuchen, N.J.: Scarecrow, 1994.

65. PEJTERSEN, A. Fiction and the library classification. *Scandinavian Public Library Quarterly*, 11 (1), 1978, 5-11.

66. YU, *and* O'BRIEN, *op cit*, 171.

67. PEJTERSEN, A. M. *and* J. AUSTIN. Fiction retrieval: experimental design and evaluation of a search system based on users value criteria, Part 1. *Journal of Documentation*, 39, 1983, 230 - 246. Part 2, *Journal of Documentation*, 40, 1984, 25-35.

68. MACEWEN, A. Where do you keep the dystopias? *Library Association Record*, 99 (1) January, 1997, 40 - 41.

69. JENNINGS *and* SEAR, How readers select fiction, *op cit.*

70. PEJTERSON, A. The bookhouse: an icon based database system of fiction retrieval in public libraries. In: Cronin, B. ed. *Marketing of library and information services*. London: Aslib, 1979, 572-591.

71. BETTS D. A. *Borrowing and the fiction reader*. London: Branch and Mobile Libraries Group of the Library Association, 1987.

6. Conclusions and recommendations

This chapter presents the conclusions of the study: from the literature survey, questionnaire responses, interviews and the seminar organized in April 1997 to discuss interim findings and the emerging issues. We also offer recommendations to central government and local authorities, the Library and Information Commission, the Arts Councils and Regional Arts Boards, the Library Association, Schools of Information and Library Studies, publishers and booksellers, and library managers.

6.1 Project aims and general conclusions

In aiming to look at adults' reading for leisure, pleasure and informal education we looked at a wide range of data - from previous studies, including user studies, the questionnaire survey, interviews and seminar discussion, and documentation gathered as part of the project. Essentially a mapping exercise, we were aware at the outset that this project's objectives were very broad, and that further in-depth work would be needed to probe some issues even further.

Our general conclusion was that reading promotion for adult users has been largely neglected, with assumptions made by library services that adult readers know what they want, read in fairly specific areas and are competent to find books for themselves or to ask specific questions when necessary. We found that it had been assumed that, on the whole, readers prefer to make their own selection without interference or influence from librarians. Librarians have tended to take a neutral stance, giving information rather than advice on reading. It was evident, though, that this is now changing. There was some activity in the majority of public libraries and many innovative and successful schemes. The task now will be for good practice to spread to all library authorities and for professionalism to be targeted more clearly on developing reading.

6.2 The service environment and the public library's role in reading promotion

A major factor which is holding back the promotion of adult reading is a lack of 'connectivity'. There is need to connect the range of promotions to the core business of libraries, and to an overall strategy for marketing the service. The turbulence of local authorities in recent years has undoubtedly affected the ability of libraries to focus sufficiently on their key objectives, but new library authority structures provide an opportunity for a re-examination of roles and priorities. The time is now right for libraries to reappraise the business they are in. There is also need now for them to connect their business to that of wider national policies for adult reading, such as adult continuing education and the lifelong learning initiative, and to ensure that reading for adults becomes part of a local authority-wide approach, as has been recommended for children in the *Investing in children* report to the then Department of National Heritage.[1] 'Badging' the concept of reading at local authority level is a challenge for librarians.

Exploiting the range of resources available and generating revenue was also a concern. There was evidence that a lack of a designated budget for reading promotion could be hampering work, even where reading promotion policy might be embedded in wider policy-making. Budgets for reading promotion were available in only one-third of authorities and, where they existed, on the whole they were so small as to make very little impact on the organization.

Lack of staff time and no specific person with responsibility were other features of this failure to recognize reading promotion as a core activity. One of the most concerning issues which has resulted from this investigation is the relationship between reading promotion and management of the service. In only 30% of library authorities was it possible to identify a member of the management team with overall responsibility for reading promotion. Sometimes this was a head of bibliographical services, sometimes the development officer or a senior post for adult lending services. Where authorities had marketing officers (26% of authorities only) only 40% of these were involved with reading promotion. There is evidence of some authorities restructuring with the aim of bringing back reader service: in one case linking bibliographical services and proactive reader development in one post, in another by decreasing the participation in stock selection thus freeing the librarian for more effective promotion. In recruitment, it seems that insufficient attention has been paid to selecting staff with knowledge or interest in books and reading, both professional and para-professional. This may have been because of priority being given to customer care or management skills, or assumptions that library staff will be natural readers. The division of staff into professional and clerical has in some cases left a gap in terms of advice to readers.

This suggests a lack of commitment from management and gives the impression that the issue is seen as peripheral. To make any real headway, it is necessary to ensure a strategic approach which involves the whole organization. As part of this, standards therefore need to be more explicit, with service plans reflecting clear targets.

We found that stock selection and reading promotion were not sufficiently pulled together. Stock policy documentation was in many cases more concerned with method than content. Devolution of selection, intended to ensure libraries reflected more accurately their communities' needs, appears not to have widened reading choice.

6.3 Reading, literature and the book world

There is a great deal of quantitative information available on what people read, how much they read and on book buying and book borrowing behaviour, particularly from Book Marketing Ltd and from the Library and Information Statistics Unit. There is also a good deal of research data on browsing, categorization and alternative arrangements: all of which have considerable practical implications for libraries, but which do not appear to have been made use of sufficiently. Dissemination and awareness of these data therefore need to be further developed.

There is, however, comparatively little research on the effects of reading on readers or how reading develops readers, despite the testimonies of many public figures, who refer to seminal books which they found at some turning point in their lives. There is a need for more qualitative research and longitudinal studies on reader development to highlight how and when librarians can support and intervene to benefit readers.

The work of the Arts Council, England, has clearly been influential in present development, in providing funding incentives which have sometimes given the 'permission to innovate' that was needed, but also the support, training and expertise which has led to librarians gaining a renewed confidence in taking a more proactive role. Literature development workers have been supportive here, although their posts have been criticized for their isolation and short term nature. Partnerships at regional level have been improving, particularly between library authorities and regional arts boards, with the Opening the Book festival an important outcome and example of this activity.

However, we found that the narrow definition of literature has meant that much of the work is fiction orientated: this is partly due to the Arts Council's influence, but also has to be seen as librarians' apparent reluctance actively to promote non-fiction for leisure reading. This pointed up the need for libraries to retain their distinctive role in relation to other cultural organizations.

6.4 Public library responses

In examining public libraries' responses to the challenges of the book trade, we noted that there was both competition in the shape of the professionalism with which book shops, especially the large retailers, relate to customers as well as direct support from book shops and library suppliers. However, clearly book buying and borrowing are not in contention: each reinforces the other. The demise of the net book agreement has not resulted in a decline in titles published, but there were implications for the level of support that library suppliers might be able to continue offering on promotion.

Borrowing from libraries continues to be significant, but we found that new/unknown authors were less likely to satisfy readers and that there was need to communicate more to readers through better targeted promotion. The role of readers' advisors may be important here, although there were mixed attitudes to this. The new readers' advisor appears to be more concerned with finding ways of maximising advice to benefit a greater number of readers than working on a one-to-one basis. However the reading promotion role is delivered, though, it was evident that staff training and education were essential. One of the main identified needs of staff is confidence in their ability to advise and help readers, and management must accept a responsibility here. Giving the staff the tools to do the job may be as simple as making available bibliographies and booklists, and providing them with research and management information on reading trends, such as that collected by Book Marketing. Without this information there may seem to be no overall pattern to books and reading and the topic can overwhelm.

The whole issue of library education and training for professional staff needs further attention. The emphasis on management and information technology in the curriculum of schools of information and library studies is largely responsible for the dilution of stock management and book knowledge. The profession is increasingly divergent and non-public library sectors probably have less interest in the content of materials and are more concerned with information retrieval. It was indeed suggested by one County librarian that we may have to face the fact that librarians can no longer be interchangeable between sectors. The Arts Council, England, has brought this back on the agenda through its pump-priming of a module specifically for students wishing to enter a career in public libraries. The needs of public libraries for continuing education and in-house training in relation to book knowledge and promotion is a matter which also needs to be addressed.

6.5 Marketing and promoting reading

Despite the range of studies into libraries marketing over recent years, and the rating by 93% of library authorities in our survey that reading promotion was 'essential, very important, or important' in only 31% was this intention translated into written policy documentation and in even fewer (18%) was there a plan. Where plans existed, these tended to be service or building based and concerned with specific activities, such as reading clubs or displays. There was little evidence of a total marketing strategy or a plan for reading promotion, integral to the overall service. It appears that reading promotion is mostly seen as an end in itself, not rooted in strategic planning and instead is sidelined to promotional activities presented in a vacuum.

In any marketing plan, segmenting the market or defining target groups is essential. In the public sector this is more difficult: there are political and legal constraints and library authorities are vulnerable to political opportunism. It is nevertheless important to clarify the targets and one authority had done this, identifying two main aims:

1. widening the reading horizons of existing users;
2. attracting non-users to the library, sub-dividing them into those who find their reading material elsewhere, e.g., book buyers, and those who are non-readers.

There is a concern that readers are now less served than non-readers and that the articulate library user may now be getting their books from elsewhere. It does appear that the majority of library promotion is targeted either at the non-user or the user of specific services like business information whereas, on the whole, reading promotion is seen as more to do with organizing events or describing particular sorts of books rather than identifying the needs of target audiences.

Evaluation of reading activities is also at an early stage: only 15% of library authorities stated that they used performance measures and examples given were quantitative rather than qualitative. The Arts Council, England, has helped to encourage evaluation by requiring this in reports on funded projects; the Audit Commission and CIPFA so far only ask for numbers of 'activities', unrelated to any objective or evaluation. Currently, user surveys appear fairly broad-brush, seldom going into any great depth about what users are hoping to find and how satisfied they are with their book choice. Whilst recognizing the delicacy of what may seem private information, much more needs to be known about reader expectations, relationships to life style behaviours and reader development. Computerized data could provide useful information, but would need to be considered in the light of data protection legislation.

Despite these reservations about promotion activities, we cite several examples of coordinated programmes and festivals where good practice can be replicated by other authorities, with need for more work in promoting non-fiction by these means. We also emphasized that promotion by libraries involves more than activity, and that shelf arrangement and support of browsing, in particular, should be targeted for action.

Research shows that a significant number of library users select their material by browsing, that they use the catalogue very little and consult the staff hardly at all. This may be because of misplaced assumptions that information desks are intended just for 'information' enquiries, or that it does not occur to them that librarians are interested in sharing their reading. Further work needs to be undertaken with users to probe this. Much of readers' selection is based on known authors, categorization - where this exists - use of the book blurb and personal recommendations. There is a need for more qualitative research on methods of promotion which might use focus groups, interviews, exit polls, qualitative questionnaires, customer satisfaction surveys and input as well as output measures, which would indicate added value. The use of IT, including the Internet, could offer ways of both promoting books and aiding information retrieval by readers.

In asking library authorities to identify future developments, we had encouraging responses, summed up in the words of one Assistant Director:

> Attitudes are changing and staff are beginning to see the importance of reading. We have the foundation stone firmly laid and now need to start building.

In offering our recommendations, we submit that this building is urgently needed, to maintain public libraries' key role as supporter and co-provider of the nation's reading environment.

6.6 Recommendations

We have targeted the recommendations to:

1. Central and Local Government
2. The Library and Information Commission
3. The Arts Councils of England, Scotland, Wales and Northern Ireland and the Regional Arts Boards

4. The Library Association
5. Schools of Information and Library Studies
6. Publishers, booksellers and library suppliers
7. Library Managers
8. The British Library

6.6.1 Policy

6.6.1.1

Strategies should be developed whereby reading can be presented to the public as a positive and active means of recreation, lifelong learning and leisure.
1 2 3 4 5 6 7 8

6.6.1.2

The development and promotion of reading for leisure, pleasure and informal education should be acknowledged and supported as a core function of public libraries by policy makers.
1 2 3 4 5 7 8

6.6.1.3

Reader services and information services should be seen as complementary and mutually supportive. Reading (including the reading of fiction) should be recognized as a means of extending and enhancing basic information and enabling people to reason and to make choices in their lives.
1 2 3 4 5 7 8

6.6.1.4

Public libraries should be proactive in developing policies and strategies for reader development and reading promotion.
1 2 3 4 7

6.6.2 Co-operation

6.6.2.1

Co-operation between agencies with a particular interest in the promotion of reading should be encouraged.
1 2 3 4 5 6 7 8

6.6.3 The Arts Councils
6.6.3.1
The Arts Councils and the Regional Arts Boards are welcomed as partners with public libraries in the promotion of reading. The agendas are understandably different but better alignment on a definition of literature and the priority given to the support of writers or readers would help cooperation and development. A stronger lead from the Arts Councils and The Library Association is called for.
3 4 7

6.6.4 A national conference
6.6.4.1
The significance of the 'Reading the future' conference as a policy and dissemination forum should be recognized and a further conference should be held in the near future.
2 3 4

6.6.5 The book trade
6.6.5.1
The experience of the book trade in terms of display and layout, stock holding and staff recruitment, training and marketing should be exploited, through means that might include joint training and seminars. Experience should also flow from libraries to the book trade.
5 6 7

6.6.6 Education and training
6.6.6.1
Recognition should be given to the needs of public libraries for librarians with basic knowledge of books, selection, reading development and promotion. Consideration should be given to the means by which this could be delivered through initial training and/or continuing education, with further pump-priming where ncessary.
2 5 6 7

6.6.6.2
It should be considered whether librarians should be seen as 'interchangeable' and whether public libraries require different education and training priorities to special and academic libraries.
2 5 7

6.6.6.3

Library managers should ensure that staff have support and training to develop reading.

7

6.6.7 Marketing

6.6.7.1.

Reading development and promotion should be viewed as integral to the work of public libraries and be developed as part of the overall marketing strategy.

1 2 3 7

6.6.7.2

Public libraries should develop marketing plans for reading development and promotion.

1 2 4 7

6.6.7.3

Medium and longer term programmes should build on previous development work.

2 4 7

6.6.7.4

Marketing research, including in- depth user studies, should be conducted to ascertain the reading needs of library users, how they choose their books and how satisfied they are with their reading.

2 5 7 8

6.6. 8 Evaluation

6.6.8.1

Consideration should be given to the development of better methods of evaluation, including the use of adequate performance indicators.

1 2 4 5 7 8

6.6.9 Budget

6.6.9.1

A budget for reading promotion and development should be established which reflects the degree of importance which is given to this area of the service. External funding including Arts Council and Regional Arts

Board, book trade and other sponsorship and the generation of income through ticket sales, etc., should be included.
1 2 7

6.6.10 Management
6.6.10.1
Public library managers should ensure that staffing structures reflect the importance of reading and reader development:

a. Responsibility for reading development is identified at management team level.
b. Posts with specialist responsibility for research and development, co-ordination, advice and training are established.
c. The expertise of staff working in bibliographical sections should be recognized.
d. The role of the marketing officer should be strengthened in relation to the marketing marketing of reading.

1 7

6.6.11 Staff
6.6.11.1
Staff should be recruited at all levels with a knowledge and enthusiasm for books and reading.
7

6.6.11.2
The role of non professional staff is recognized. It should be clear what is expected of them in giving advice and help to readers in their choice of books. Appropriate training should be given.
7

6.6.11.3
Librarians need to acknowledge a proactive role in helping readers to widen their choice of reading and opening out areas of stock which might otherwise go unnoticed.
7

6.6.12 Research

6.6.12.1

Research into reading development and reading promotion should be commissioned, including longitudinal studies in reader development and the most effective ways in which readers can be helped to become more informed.

2 4 5 7 8

6.6.13 Alternative arrangements

6.6.13.1

Public Libraries should consider the use of alternative arrangements, display, categorization, face-on shelving as a means of promoting reading and presenting readers with an easier way to select their reading materials. Further research into this is needed.

4 5 7 8

6.6.13.2

Investigation should be undertaken into a compatible stock categorization system which would be practical and realistic for libraries to implement, and also the means by which more 'blurbs' could be produced - using informed reviews.

4 5 7 8

6.6.14 A national marketing agency

6.6.14.1

The bid for a national marketing agency should be noted and should be supported. If this is unsuccessful other means should be investigated into ways of putting this into practice.

1 2 4 7

Reference

1. LIBRARY AND INFORMATION SERVICES COUNCIL (ENGLAND) WORKING PARTY ON LIBRARY SERVICES FOR CHILDREN AND YOUNG PEOPLE. *Investing in children: the future of library services for children and young people.* London: HMSO, 1995.

Select bibliography

Ainley, P. and B. Totterdell. *Alternative arrangements: new approaches to public library stock.* London: Association of Assistant Librarians,1982.

Alster, L. Bibliotekscentraleni: The Danish Library Bureau. *Scandinavian Public Libraries Quarterly*, 1(4) 1968, 226 - 238

Baker, S. L. Book lists: what we know, what we need to know. RQ, Winter, 1993, 171-180.

Baker, S.L.. The display phenomenon: an exploration into factors causing the increased circulation of displayed books. Library Quarterly, 56, 1986, 237-257.

Baker, S. L. *The responsive public library collection. How to develop and market it.* Colorado: Libraries Unlimited, 1993.

Baker, S. I. What patrons read and why: the link between personality and reading, In: Grenier, J.M., ed. *Research issues in public libraries: trends for the future.* New York: Greenwood Press, 1996.

Baker, S. L. Will fiction classification schemes increase use? RQ , 27 (3), 1988, 366-376.

Baker, S. L. Why book displays increase use: a review of causal factors. *Public Libraries,* 25 (2), 1986, 63 - 65.

Baverstock, A. *How to market books.* London: Kegan Paul, 1993.

Baverstock, A. *Are books different? Marketing and the book trade.* London: Kegan Paul, 1993.

Brewis, W. L. E., E. M. Gericke and J. A. Kruger. Reading needs and motives of adult users of fiction. *Mousaion*, 12 (2), 1994. 3-18.

Bushing, M. C. The library's product and excellence. *Library Trends*, 43 (3), 1995, 384-400.

Capital Planning Information. *Promoting reading: libraries and literature. Library and Information policies seminar 10th November, 1994.* Stamford: Capital Planning Information, 1994.

Comedia. *Borrowed Time? The future of public libraries in the U K.* Stroud: Comedia, 1993.

Corns, I. J. A Study into fiction classification and categorization. MA dissertation Loughborough University Department of Information and Library Studies, 1995.

Cronin, B. Nationally co-ordinated library promotion. Journal of Librarianship , 13, 1981, 2231.

Denham, D. Back to basics: training and educational opportunities of the exploitation of fiction in Public libraries. *Public Library Journal,* 11(3), 1996, 77-80.

Dixon, J. *Fiction in Libraries.* London: Library Association Publishing, 1986.

England, L. *Borrowing books. Readership and library usage in Great Britain.* London: British Library, 1992. (British National Bibliography Research Fund Report 59) Evans, B. and S. Edwards. Well worth reading; fiction promotion in three authorities. *Public Library Journal*, 3(4), 1988, 75- 78.

Goldhor, H. The effects of prime display location on public library circulation of selected adult titles. *Library Quarterly*, 42, 1972, 371-389.

Goldhor, H. Experimental effects on the choice of books borrowed by public library adult patrons. *Library Quarterly*, 51, 1981, 253-268.

Goodall, D. *Browsing in public libraries.* Loughborough: Loughborough University Library and Information Statistics Unit, 1989.

Goodall, D. Improving access to European fiction. *Library and Information Research News*, 16(56), 1993,18 - 20.

Greenhalgh, L. and K. Worpole with C. Landry. *Libraries in a world of cultural change.* London: UCL, 1995.

Hamshere, S. Exploration and escape; the needs fulfilled by borrowing books from the public library. MA dissertation , Sheffield University Department of Information Studies, 1996.

Hatt, F. *The reading process: a framework for analysis and description.* London: Bingley, 1976.

Hawking, J. New fiction, adult education and the library. *Public Library Quarterly*, 4(1), 1983, 42-53.

Heeks, P. *Public libraries and the arts: an evolving partnership.* London: Library Association, 1989.

Hermenze, J. The classics will circulate. *Library Journal*, 106, Nov 15, 1981, 2191-2195.

Hicks, D. *Research project to develop and implement a proposal for an accredited literature module for librarianship courses.* London: Arts Council of England, 1995 .

Hughes, V. M. *Literature belongs to everyone. A report on widening access to literature.* London: Arts Council of Great Britain, 1991.

Huse, R. and J. Huse, ed. *Who else writes like.? A guide to fiction authors.* Loughborough: Loughborough University Library and Information Statistics Unit, 1996.

Ings, R. *Report on the literature development worker movement in England.* London: The Arts Council of Great Britain, 1992.

Jennings, B. and L. Sear. How readers select fiction: a survey in Kent. *Public Library Journal*, 1(4), 1986, 43 - 47.

Jennings, B. and L. Sear. Novel ideas: a browsing area for fiction,. *Public Library Journal,* 4(3), 1989, 41 - 44.

Karetsky, S. *Reading research and librarianship.* New York: Greenwood Press, 1982.

Kempthorne, B. Still well worth reading about: Well worth reading - the third chapter. *Public Library Journal*, 6(6), 1991, 157 - 161.

King, I. *Promote! The Handbook of Public Library Promotions.* London: Public Libraries Group of the Library Association, 1989.

Kinnell, M., ed. *Managing fiction in libraries.* London: Library Association Publishing, London, 1991.

Kinnell, M. and J. MacDougall. *Meeting the marketing challenge: strategies for public libraries and leisure services.* London: Taylor Graham, 1994.

Kotler, P. and A. Andreasen, A. *Strategic marketing for non profit organizations.* EnglewoodCliffs, NJ: Prentice-Hall, 1987.

Library and Information Services Council (England) Working Party on Library Services for Children and Young People. *Investing in children: the future of library services for children and young people.* London: HMSO, 1995.

Luckham, B. How constant are the readers? In: Kaegbein, P., B. Luckham and V Stelmach, eds. *Studies on research in reading and libraries.* Paris: K.G. Saur, 1991.

McKearney, M. Well worth reading: fiction promotion scheme comes of age. *Public Library Journal*, 5(3), 1990, 61 - 67.

Mann, M. *The reading habits of adults: a select annotated bibliography.* London: British Library, 1977 (British National Bibliography Research Fund Report No.1)

Mann, P. H. *Back to books: papers given at the Public Libraries Group of the Library Association weekend school held at Loughborough University of Technology March, 1985.* London: Public Libraries Group, 1985.

Mann, P .H, *Books: buyers and borrowers.* London: Deutsch, 1971.

Mann, P. H. *From author to reader: a social study of books.* London: Routledge and Kegan Paul, 1982.

Mann, P. H. *The literary novel and its public. Report to the Arts Council Literature Panel.* Sheffield: University of Sheffield, 1980.

Marriott, R. How well do libraries inform their public? *Library Association Record,* 95(3) 1993,164 - 167.

Nell, V. *Lost in a book; the psychology of reading for pleasure.* New Haven: Yale University Press, 1988.

O`Rourke, R. *Unpopular readers: The case for genre fiction. Working Paper 7.* Stroud: Comedia, 1993.

Phelan, K. *Libraries and reading promotion schemes. Working Paper 5.* Stroud: Comedia, 1993.

Pyle, J. Publicity and promotion. In: *British Librarianship and Information work 1981-1985.*

London: Library Association, 1988, 219 -229.

Pyle, J. Publicity and promotion. In: *British Librarianship and Information work 1986-1990.* London: Library Association, 1992, 199 - 207.

Ross, C. S. Readers` advisory service: new directions. *RQ,* 30 (4) 1991, 503-518.

Sabine, G. and P. *Books that made a difference, what people told us.* New York: Library Professional Publications, 1983.

Sear, L. and B. Jennings. *How readers select fiction.* Kent County Council, County Library Research and Development report. Maidstone: Kent County Council, 1986.

Sear , L. and Jennings, B. *Novel ideas: a browsing area for fiction.* Kent County Library Research and Development report No.10. Maidstone: Kent County Council, 1989.

Simsova, S. Nicholas Rubakin and Bibliopsychology, *Libri,* 16, 1966,118 - 29. Reprinted In: Simsova, S. and Kujoth, J. S.eds. *Readers and book selection .* Metuchen, NJ: Scarecrow Press, 1969.

Spenceley, N. The readership of literary fiction : a survey of library users in the Sheffield Area.MA dissertation, Sheffield University Department of Information Studies, 1989.

Spiller, D. The provision of fiction for public libraries, *Journal of Librarianship* ,12 (4), 1980, 238 - 266.

Stewart, I. *Shelf talk: promoting literature in public libraries.* London: The Arts Council of England / The Library Association, 1996.

Sweetland, J.H. Adult fiction in medium sized U.S. public libraries: a survey, *Library Resources and Technical Services,* 38 (2), 1994, 149 - 160.

Tasker, J. and Shepherd, J. eds. *Words across Europe partnership. Report and recommendations.* Northampton: Northamptonshire County Library Service, 1997.

Usherwood, R . *Success stories : libraries are full of them.* Sheffield: Yorkshire and Humberside Branch of the Library Association, 1993.

Van Riel, R. and Fowler, O. *Opening the book : finding a good read.* Bradford: Bradford Libraries, 1996.

Van Riel, R. *Reading the future; a place for literature in public libraries. A report of the seminar held in York 2nd and 3rd March 1992 organized by the Arts Council of Great Britain in association with the Library Association and the Regional Arts Boards of England .* London: The Library Association, 1992.

Van Riel, R. The case for fiction, *Public Library Journal,* 8 (3), 1993, 81 - 84.

Walters, R. The library, the bookshop and the literature centre. *New Library World,* 96 1995, 21 - 27.

Warren, G. Reading across Europe (The Seals Project). *Public Library Journal,* 11(4), 1996, 97- 100.

Warren, G. *Developing together in literature promotion. An evaluation of collaborative training for public library staff in the West Midlands, 1995-6.* Birmingham: West Midlands Regional Library System. 1996.

Wiegard, W. A. Taste cultures and librarians: a position paper. *Drexel Library Quarterly*, 16(3), 1980, 1-11.

Willard, P. and V. Teece. The browser and the library. *Public Library Quarterly*, Sydney, Australia, 1983, 55-63.

Worpole, K. *The public library and the bookshop. Working Paper 3.* Stroud: Comedia, 1993.

Worpole, K, and C. Landry. *Libraries in a world of cultural change.* London: UCL Press, 1995.

Yu, L. and A. O'Brien. Domain of adult fiction librarianship. *Advances in Librarianship*, 20 1996, 151-189.

ADULT READING PROMOTION IN PUBLIC LIBRARIES

Questionnaire for Chief Librarians

Please tick boxes as appropriate

POLICY

1. Does your Library Service have a written statement of
    aims/objectives on the promotion of adult reading (either a
    separate document or incorporated in the library's overall
    policy document)?

    Yes ☐
    No ☐

    If so we would be grateful if you could attach a copy to this
    questionnaire.

2. Is there a specific plan relating to reading promotion?

    Yes ☐
    No ☐

    If yes, how often is the plan revised?

    annually ☐
    2-3 years ☐
    other ☐
    (please specify)

We would welcome any documentation on this.

3. How would you rate reading promotion in relation to other
    priorities in your service?

    essential ☐
    very important ☐
    important ☐
    not particularly
    important ☐
    a waste of
    resources ☐

4. Does reading promotion feature in any performance indicators
    you may use?

    Yes ☐
    No ☐

    If yes please give examples

5.   Have you undertaken any user studies into any of the following?   Yes   No

   1. How readers choose their books   ☐   ☐
   2. Evaluation of methods of reading promotion for adults   ☐   ☐
   3. Book selection related to reading promotion   ☐   ☐
   4. Other relevant user studies   ☐   ☐

Any documentation on user studies of relevance would be welcomed.

STAFF

6.   Within your library service's management team is there a
     post with overall responsibility for reading promotion?   Yes   ☐
                                                                     No   ☐
     If so please name post ....

7.   Is there a specific post responsible for reading promotion throughout
     the service?   Yes   ☐
                                                                     No   ☐
     If yes please name post ....
     We would be grateful for a copy of the job description.

8.   Does your library service have a Marketing Officer?   Yes   ☐
                                                                     No   ☐

     If yes is reading promotion part of their role?   Yes   ☐
                                                                     No   ☐

9.   Do any of your libraries have a specific post of Readers' Advisor?   Yes   ☐
                                                                           No   ☐
     If yes we would be grateful for a copy of the job description.

10. Is any provision made for training staff in reading promotion?   Yes   ☐
                                                                        No   ☐

     If yes is this provided?   in-house   ☐
                                                       externally   ☐
                                                       both   ☐

Please indicate subjects of training and tick all that apply

organisation/marketing of events ☐
readers' advisory role in reading promotion ☐
positive attitudes to reading promotion ☐
evaluation/selection of materials linked to promotion ☐
knowledge of stock ☐

BUDGET

11 Is there a specific budget for reading promotion in your services? Yes ☐
No ☐

If yes please give approximate amount   -£1000 ☐
£1000-£2000 ☐
£5000 + ☐

LIBRARY LAYOUT

12. Do any of your libraries incorporate any of the following facilities?
Please tick boxes as appropriate.
Rank the 3 you see as most important in promoting reading.

Rank 3 most important (1,2,3)

☐ dumpbins ☐
☐ face on display ☐
☐ laid out browsing area ☐
☐ catergorization ☐
☐ annotated OPAC ☐
☐ Hypertext/CD-ROM selection aids ☐
☐ guiding as a selection aid ☐
☐ printed bibliographical tools for public use ☐
☐ other (please specify) ☐

....

....

BOOK SELECTION

13.   What is your major aim in book selection?
      Please tick one.

      to cater for all tastes ☐

      emphasis is given to new titles likely to be in demand ☐

      emphasis is given to what will issue well ☐

      we look for books which will complement existing collections ☐

      we ensure that selection includes important titles which might
      not fit the stereotype of the average reader ☐

      other (please specify) ....

      ....

      ....

      If you have a book selection policy please attach.

14.   Do you use

      CD-ROM ☐
      approval service ☐
      other (please specify) ☐

      ....

      ....

READING PROMOTION INITIATIVES

15.   Has your library service been involved with any of the following reading
      promotions initiatives over the last year (1995-96)?

      Programme of author visits ☐
      Literature festival ☐
      Preparation of booklists/reading guides ☐

Circulating displays ☐
Competitions ☐
Other (please specify) ☐

....

....

READING PROMOTION DEVELOPMENT

16. Please give your opinion on the following statements.
Please tick appropriate box.

	strongly agree			strongly disagree	
	1	2	3	4	5
Reading promotion is a core activity	☐	☐	☐	☐	☐
To foster the reading habit should be a key task for librarians	☐	☐	☐	☐	☐
Advising readers in their choice of books should be included in job descriptions of front line staff	☐	☐	☐	☐	☐
Librarians underestimate the reading potential of the public	☐	☐	☐	☐	☐
'...the self effacing culture of librarians can lead to assumptions that librarians are...without opinions or values of their own' (Comedia Report)	☐	☐	☐	☐	☐
We would make more impact by promoting recommended books than by promoting books/library services in general	☐	☐	☐	☐	☐
It would be preferable for librarians to spend less time in selection and more in promotion	☐	☐	☐	☐	☐
What we need is a national marketing agency similar to the Dutch N.B.L.C.	☐	☐	☐	☐	☐

17. In the last year have you been involved in any joint initiatives
in adult reading promotion? Yes ☐
No ☐

If yes was this with:

other library services	☐
library suppliers	☐
local bookshops	☐
regional arts board	☐
other (please specify)	☐

....

....

Please decribe briefly the nature of the joint initiative.

18.   Do you subscribe to Shelf Talk?   Yes ☐ No ☐

If yes how is it used ....

....

....

ARTS COUNCIL INITIATIVES

19.   With which Regional Arts Board are you linked? ....

20.   Is there a Regional Arts/library literature development policy in your region?   Yes ☐ No ☐

If so we would be grateful for a copy.

21.   Is there a Literature Development Worker?   Yes ☐ No ☐

If yes is he/she library based?   Yes ☐ No ☐

22.   Has your library service received Arts Council funding for literature development initiatives?   Yes ☐ No ☐

APPENDIX

If yes please briefly describe scheme/s

In 1993/4

In 1994/5

In 1995/6

We would welcome documentation on any schemes noted.

THE READER, LIBRARIES AND BOOKSHOPS

Please give your opinion on the following statements:

'The public library will be unable to compete with the commercial bookshops activities because:

	strongly agree 1	2	3	strongly disagree 4	5
1. The ambience of the bookshops is preferable	☐	☐	☐	☐	☐
2. The public feel they can ask for help in selection	☐	☐	☐	☐	☐
3. The trade know what is of current interest	☐	☐	☐	☐	☐
4. Bookshops attract....staff recruited on the basis of their enthusiasm for books and ideas' (Comedia Report)	☐	☐	☐	☐	☐

23. Are there any particular constraints in the promotion of books to
     adult readers?   Yes ☐
                                                               No ☐

     If yes please indicate importance by ranking in boxes (no.1 as the
     greatest constraint and so on):

     objectives are decided by a committee who do

     not see this as a priority   ☐

     no specific person responsible   ☐

     no specific budget   ☐

     lack of staff time   ☐

     staff attitudes   ☐

     lack of performance measures   ☐

     other (please specify)   ☐

     ....

24. Please give an indication of opportunities for reading promotion in your authority in the
     future if you feel this is likely to become possible.

     A number of authorities will be invited to take part in a follow-up interview.
     If you are willing to take part in the second stage of this project, please indicate
     by ticking the box.   ☐

     If yes who would be the most appropriate person to contact in the first instance?

     ....
     Thank you very much for your time and co-operation

     Please return by 28th November 1996 to:
     Carolyn Pritchett
     Department of Information and Library Studies
     Loughborough University
     Loughborough
     Leicestershire
     LE11 3TU

     To whom enquiries should also be addressed
     Telephone 01509 - 223059
     Fax 01509 - 223053